Accelerated Learning Techniques

2 Manuscripts –

Mind Hacking and Memory Improvement

Accelerated Learning Techniques

2 Manuscripts –

Mind Hacking and Memory Improvement

Advanced Strategies to Learn Faster, Be More Productive, Improve Memory, and Unlock Your Full Potential

Kyle Faber

Accelerated Learning Techniques: 2 Manuscripts – Mind Hacking and Memory Improvement

Copyright © 2019 Kyle Faber

All rights reserved. No portion of this book may be reproduced, stored in a retrieval system, or transmitted in any form or by any means – electronic, mechanical, photocopy, recording, scanning, or other – except for brief quotations in critical reviews or articles, without prior written permission of the publisher.

Published by CAC Publishing LLC

ISBN: 978-1-950010-21-9 paperback

ISBN: 978-1-950010-20-2 eBook

Table of Contents

Mind Hacking 11

  Introduction: The Untapped Potential of the Most Powerful Tool 16

  Chapter 1: What Is "Hacking" Your Mind? 18

    Activity 1: Start a journal 24

  Chapter 2: You Becoming the Director of Your Mind 26

    The "monkey mind" 26

    Activity 2.1: Observe the monkey mind 30

    Garbage in garbage out 32

    Activity 2.2: Observe the inputs 33

  Chapter 3: The Mind's Codes 35

    "Buggy" code – how you got it 36

    Debugging the code 39

      Loops 39

      Habits 43

      Discipline & effort, resonance & momentum 48

    Eliminating unnecessary distractions 53

    If-Then loops 55

Activity 3: Identify your habits, good & bad 57

Chapter 4: Fundamental Loops and Virtual Models 58

Activity 4.1: Rooting out the fundamental loop: the "Why?" exercise 59

Virtual models, self & self-image 61

Activity 4.2: Journal the gap between virtual and actual 68

Chapter 5: Beyond the Cognitive 70

The "extrasensory" you 72

Activity 5.1: Breathe into Focus 74

Hacking for "psychic" powers 75

#1: Write it down 78
#2: Talk less 78
#3: Concentrate & pay attention 79
#4: Wake up before 5 a.m. 80

Activity 5.2: Concentration exercises 81

#1: Observe and remember 81
#2: Listen 82
#3: Memorize 82
#4: Notice distractions 82

Chapter 6: Blueprinting Your Mind 84

Activity 6.1: Journaling for a purpose 84

Conflicting directions 85

Blueprinting a new habit 91

Activity 6.2: Journal for supporting values 92

Chapter 7: The Body's Contribution to the Mind 94

The body's economy of effort and energy.. 95

Activity 7: Gratitude hack 98

Chapter 8: Hacking the Tangible Brain 99

The brain 101

The cells of the brain 104

Six hacks for the physical brain 106

Your brain is only as good as what you eat 106

Get more oxygen to your brain 110

    Breathe better 111

    Circulation and absorption 113

    1. Drink plenty of water 115

    2. Increase blood volume 118

    3. Work out more 118

Sleep better 119

Get some sunshine every day 123

Afterword 125

Memory Improvement 128

Introduction: An Evolving Memory 133

The evolution of the brain 136

The evolution of memory 137
Chapter 1: The Brain, Neurons, and Memory
.... 143
　The birth of neurons: *neurogenesis* 146
　The death of neurons: *neuroapoptosis* 150
　The living and changing brain: *neuroplasticity* 151
　Setting the stage for a better memory 155
Chapter 2: The Making of Memories 159
　Photographic memory 165
　Memory encoding 167
Chapter 3: Visualization 174
Chapter 4: Memory Pegs 181
Chapter 5: Memory Palace Method 190
Chapter 6: The Neuroplastic Brain 196
　Memory and neuroplasticity 196
　Exercise: Write out your intention 200
　Exercise: Flash photo memory 202
　Exercise: Beethoven's neuron-building *Ninth* 203
Chapter 7: Emotion & Memory 206
Chapter 8: Mindfulness, Meditation, and Reflection 211
　Mindfulness and the "monkey mind" 212

    Meditation 221

    Reflection 225

    Frequency 226

Chapter 9: Fading Memory, Diet, Exercise, and Sleep 228

    Eating and drinking 229

    Working out 231

    Sleep 233

Conclusion 237

Mind Hacking

How to Unleash the Full Potential of Your Brain to Achieve Anything You Want

Mind Hacking

How to Unleash the Full Potential of Your Brain to Achieve Anything You Want

Unlock the Secrets of Your Brain and Become the Director of Your Own Life

Kyle Faber

Mind Hacking - How to Unleash the Full Potential of Your Brain to Achieve Anything You Want

Unlock the Secrets of Your Brain and Become the Director of Your Own Life

Copyright © 2018 Kyle Faber

All rights reserved. No portion of this book may be reproduced, stored in a retrieval system, or transmitted in any form or by any means – electronic, mechanical, photocopy, recording, scanning, or other – except for brief quotations in critical reviews or articles, without prior written permission of the publisher.

Published by CAC Publishing LLC

ISBN: 978-1-950010-09-7 paperback

ISBN: 978-1-950010-08-0 eBook

Introduction: The Untapped Potential of the Most Powerful Tool

A substantial part of human history has simply been about the human quest for ever more powerful and useful tools. Just think of all the things in the world that have been developed by the human mind. From harnessing fire to inventing the wheel, from Guttenberg's printing press to the Adobe PDF on your screen, so many human inventions, developments, and creations have been about creating tools to extend human abilities. Even AI, artificial intelligence, which mimics the human brain, is only another tool.

And yet, you already have the most powerful tool of all, the human mind. It has the power to create such advanced tools, and you already own one of those minds, but, like most, you probably haven't been getting the full benefit of it and what it is capable of. It's like walking into Harry Potter's wand shop on Diagon Alley and getting your hands on Professor Dumbledore's twin wand. Once you have the wand, you need to control it. And that is what "hacking" your mind is all about.

Your mind is the most powerful tool of all, or at least it has the potential to be. Mind hacking isn't about attaching an external electronic prosthesis to the brain and adding value to it from the outside. The mind has untapped powers that far exceed anything you could possibly contribute through any electronic attachment. Imagine what would happen if we spent the same resources to hack the human mind as we have in developing technologies and AI. The benefits would be significant and widespread. That's what we are doing here in this book. We are attempting to advance the potential of the human mind.

Chapter 1: What Is "Hacking" Your Mind?

Let me start by posing a simple question: What is *I*?

Before you think that's a typo, that I didn't have a good proofreader check my book, let me say, "What is I?" is precisely what I mean. And it's a very different question than "Who am I?" I'm not looking for you to provide a list of personal qualities or for you to define your identity.

So, let's ask it again. "What is I?"

I pose the question that way because you undoubtedly refer to yourself as "I." My question is simple – just what is it that you are referring to as "I"? If you want to hack your own mind, then the *you* that does the hacking is different than the *you* that is the mind that is to be hacked. This point can't be overstated. It is the key to everything we do in this book.

Imagine a car saying, if a car could, "I want to fix my engine," or a computer saying, "I will turn on." A computer that can turn itself on is one that is in standby mode on a different circuit whose job is to do just one thing – turn the computer on. In other words, the computer turning itself on isn't really the full complement of the computer turning itself on – it's turned on by a separate component sitting in the background.

When someone says they want to hack their own mind, it is not their mind that is saying that, is it? The mind can't possibly say it's going to hack itself. That would be like your computer hacking your computer. When you say you want to wake up at 4 a.m., who is the one that doesn't allow that to happen? When you want to go on a diet, who is suggesting that? "What is *I*?"

The obvious conclusion is that you and your mind are two different entities. *You* are not *your mind*. By picking up a copy of a book about hacking your mind, you are tacitly in agreement with that, although you may not have realized it.

You are not *your mind*. So, when I ask, "What is *I*?" I am asking you to think about what or who it is that you are referring to whenever you say, "*I* want this," "*I* love that," and "*I* want to hack my mind." Every time you say "*I*," just who or what does that *I* represent?

Let's look at this another way. If you are a movie buff, as I was when I was much younger, you know there are two kinds of movie-watching experiences. During one, you become so engrossed in the movie that you don't really detect the errors in logic or the bloopers. The opposite occurs when you can't seem to get into the movie, and you remain a spectator, observing from the outside. You see everything, not because you are a critic, but because you are seeing the overall movie. You haven't gotten into one character's experience or been pulled into the movie. I never notice the flaws in any movie I am truly engrossed in. But if I'm not interested, or the movie hasn't captured me, I can find all sorts of bloopers. Are you like that too?

When you are engrossed in the movie, you are *in* the movie, but when you are able to see all the little flaws and bloopers, you are watching *over* the movie. Do you get the spatial analogy? In the first kind of movie watching experience, you become part of the movie, you are *in* it, forgetting your actual physical location and becoming part of that movie's reality. In the second, you remain *outside* the movie, with a bird's eye view of all that goes on.

You and *your mind* have the same relationship. You become so engrossed with what your mind does that you think you *are* your mind, but you are not. You are simply caught up *in* the movie that is playing in your mind and engrossed by it. Most of us are so deep into our mind's perception of the outside reality that we don't realize the distinct difference between *the mind* and the *I*, confusing the two.

However, if you think that *you* can hack *your mind* – as evidenced by your interest in this book – that suggests that you do recognize their separateness, at least intuitively. Or you may be familiar with any one of the Old World philosophies or New Age practices that seek to highlight and teach the separate nature of the *I* and *the mind*.

Now that we have an idea of who the different players are in this endeavor – the *I* and *the mind* – we will be able to assign different roles to those players as we start working with the nature of the mind to "hack" it to do what we want it to do.

Hacking is a process and a method of *working around* the design, utility, and limitations of a tool.

Let me give you an example of what I mean by "hacking," as the term is used in this book. It's like taking out an angle grinder, and instead of using it as a grinder, jerry-rigging it to a stand and using it as a circular saw. That act of rigging a contraption to allow you to use the angle grinder in a way it wasn't designed for is what "hacking" is all about.

As it pertains to your mind, "hacking" is about getting your mind to do things the mind doesn't know it can do or isn't doing, things that *you* want it to do.

Your mind is extremely powerful. So is your brain. By the way, they are two different things. Later in the book, we will focus on optimizing the physical brain. For now, just know that the brain is the physical object, and the mind is built within that. *You* are distinct from both – *the mind* and *the brain*.

The brain can physically carry out the mind's directions by moving muscles, altering metabolic rates, and doing an untold number of other things just to make those directives happen. Consider the simple act of smiling. When the mind directs a smile, the brain sends signals to a bunch of muscles. Here are some of them:

- The *levator labii superioris* pulls the corner of lip and nose up.
- The *zygomaticus major* and *minor* pull the corners of the mouth up.
- The *levator anguli oris* assist in raising the angle of mouth.
- The *risorius* pulls the corners of the mouth to the side of the face.
- The *orbicularis oculi* causes the eyes to crinkle.

Your mind sends one instruction – SMILE. Your *brain* signals multiple muscles of your *body* to do their thing, none of which you are conscious of.

In the same way that your mind tells the brain what to do, and the brain goes about and does it, *you* can tell *your mind* what to do. *You* can decide to smile. In most cases, your mind will get to work and do it. But not always.

The mind is often referred to as a "monkey mind" as it takes off on its own doing random and seemingly incongruent things. There is nothing wrong with your mind – that is its nature – and that nature is, in fact, one of the reasons it is such a powerful tool. The mind's ability to associate things is, as the saying goes, a feature not a bug. It's just that that powerful tool needs direction.

Have you seen one of those cartoons where a fireman's hose gets loose and thrashes about uncontrollably with the sheer force of the stream of water coming out? No one would consider that stream of water to be useless. In fact, it is extremely powerful. But it has no direction.

The mind is the same way – it is very powerful, but it has no direction. That's where you come into play. *You* need to give *your mind* its direction, and when it doesn't give you what you want, that is when you might "hack" it to work around its natural design and limitations. That is what hacking your mind is about – getting that infinitely powerful mind of yours to do something you want it to do, even when it isn't complying or doesn't understand.

* * *

There will be practice exercises at the end of every chapter to help you build your ability to "hack" your mind and get it to do what you want it to do.

Activity 1: Start a journal

Get a notebook that you can write in as a sort of journal. Your first entry will be to write your answers to the following questions.

1. If you were able to enhance your mind, which of the following areas would you choose to improve right now (before reading this book)?

    a. Empathy

    b. Focus

    c. Resolve

    d. Discipline

    e. Foresight

    f. Creativity

2. If you could do whatever you wanted with $100,000,000, how would you spend it?

3. What three habits would you like to stop?

4. What three habits would you like to acquire?

5. What do you want your legacy to be?

6. What will your greatest achievement this year be?

Write your answers to these questions in your journal. Also record the date and where you were.

This exercise is just to get you started on thinking about what you really want your mind to be doing and the direction you want to go in as you start to hack your mind.

Chapter 2: You Becoming the Director of Your Mind

The "monkey mind"

Meditation counselors refer to the mind that wants to do other things when you try to make it concentrate or do something specific as the "monkey mind." You will agree that the analogy is apt as you picture a monkey erratically, excitedly, and unpredictably jumping from one branch to another.

The characteristics and behaviors of the human mind are determined by the brain that underlies it. We retain memories and store information catalogued against each other in the way that the brain is designed to do. Mental content is stored in the brain by connecting electrochemical cells (neurons) with each other, allowing you to associate things from one to the other very rapidly. Computers catalog things in serial order, whereas the human mind catalogs and stores them associatively, by association.

Therefore, there are two types of thoughts that roll around in your head, one willed, the other associative. Willed thoughts are those ones that you actively seek out, the thoughts that you bring up and direct. For instance, you might deliberately call up thoughts about the kind of birthday cake you want to surprise your spouse with. By contrast, associative thoughts occur when you happen to see a nice birthday cake with an ornament on it, and that reminds you of your spouse's interest. That triggers another thought, "Hey, maybe that'd be a nice birthday cake for my honey's birthday," and off you go on a train of associative thoughts.

The problem arises when you try to think of something deliberately, purposefully putting various thoughts together, but everything you do triggers unrelated thoughts. In other words, associative thoughts are getting in the way of the willed thoughts you are trying to direct. While the distracting thoughts may not be related to what you are trying to do, they are associatively related by the words and features of the issue.

For example, you could be trying to decide on a dish for dinner, and you think of having fish. That might trigger a thought of fingers (from fish fingers). From fingers you get to thumbs. From thumbs you get thumbs-up which looks like a "like" symbol. From the like symbol, you begin to think of Facebook, and the next thing you know, you're thinking of something you saw on Facebook.

From fish to a Facebook meme. Imagine that.

Sometimes, the associative train of thoughts is conscious, and you can see the progression, but, at other times, your thoughts are not conscious to you at all. They move under the surface of conscious thought. All you realize is that you're thinking of what's for dinner one minute and the next you find yourself checking your Facebook feed.

It's like the monkey in the mind jumps out at you, and yells, "SURPRISE!!" holding a bunch of shiny and interesting thoughts. Eventually, we can even become addicted to these random thoughts because they are interesting and unexpected. For many people, those unbidden thoughts can also cause discomfort, fear, or worry. Whether negative or positive, those thoughts are still distracting *you* from what you want to do, and can, therefore, be considered intrusive. Even a favorite neighbor who keeps surprising you with wonderful stuff can become annoying when you are trying to get the baby to sleep or trying to prepare your taxes.

Intrusive thoughts vary in intensity, frequency, and by the individual. Sometimes those intrusive thoughts get so loud or insistent that the original thoughts are overwhelmed and driven out. Even though you still need to think about getting dinner ready, your thoughts are now on something you saw on Facebook, and then onto other stuff you have associated with it in your own mind. All the while *you* are along for the ride. Meantime, you can't seem to get your head in the game to prepare dinner as you keep going off on the associative rides your mind keeps taking.

At this point, you have already accomplished the first step to get out of this. What you needed to know is that *you* are not *your mind*. It takes some effort, but, knowing that, you can step back from your mind to see it from that aerial view to understand all the things happening in your own mind as they happen. You can stop being an actor immersed in the scene and become the director who has the overview of the entire scene in the context of the plot and all the rest of the elements of the movie.

Once you get used to seeing yourself as independent of your mind, you will be capable of extraordinary things, some of which can even seem inspired beyond the ordinary cognitive powers of the brain. Your mind, under good direction from *you*, can accomplish amazing objectives. For that reason, recognizing that *you* are separate and distinct from *your mind* is the first hack and most important of this book.

Successful people have mastered the ability to step back and pan out. They see both the macro and the micro views. Those who aren't able to step back to observe the workings of their own minds end up resorting to strict discipline to try to get their minds to do what they need it to do. But that is the harder and less effective way to accomplish things.

You need to develop the ability to distinguish *you* from *your mind*. Of course, they merge back together easily, even automatically, as you would want them to. The goal is to be able to choose to be the director or the actor depending on the circumstance. So, the art you want to perfect is the ability to separate out *you* from *your mind* at will, allowing them to resolve back into "one" when you no longer need to be outside the movie of your mind. Both perspectives can be fun.

The best way to separate out *the mind* is to use a little mental jujitsu. The point of jujitsu is to use the momentum and energy of the opponent and flip it around on them, using as little energy of your own as possible. You can do the same with your own thoughts. You can use them to get your own footing and establish your point of perspective toward them.

Activity 2.1: Observe the monkey mind

Find yourself a comfortable spot. Sit down quietly, without any outside distractions or demands on your time or attention. One good time to do this is after the family has gone to bed. No phone, text email updates. Just you.

Close your eyes and let your thoughts fly. If you have nothing to think about, think about anything that happened at work or what happened with the kids or your friends. Anything!

Trigger a train of thought, any kind of train of thought, and, as the thoughts start to catch on, simply step back and watch.

Watch your thoughts coming and going wherever they come from and in whatever form they take. It doesn't matter if they are serious or fantastical, from aliens at Disneyland to mathematical equations or your neighbor's latest car purchase. It doesn't matter where your mind wanders. Just watch it. And tell yourself, "Hmm. That's interesting." But don't interfere with your thoughts. Don't egg them on, stop them, question them. Don't be affected by your thoughts one way or the other. Let your thoughts pop up like Whack-a-Mole – just don't take a swing.

You will find that this exercise will give you the best proof that *you* are not *your mind*, and that you are certainly not your thoughts.

Even though you can get your mind to think the thoughts you want to think about much of the time, you will still find your mind doing its own thing. Some folks will tell you that discipline is the key. But there are "hacks" that can help you work around this feature of your mind.

As you move forward, continue to do this sit-down exercise, letting your thoughts do what they want while you simply observe them. The key is for you not to participate in your thoughts. Remember that *you* are a spectator of *your mind* and that it is not you that is doing the thinking.

You should do this daily until you begin to easily see the distinction between you and your mind. When you do, you'll be able to start observing your mind in a way that is only possible if you are outside looking in, not when you are caught up in it.

Garbage in garbage out

The mind is like an echo chamber. Give your mind one sound bite, and it will reverberate into the farthest recesses of your mind. So, what is the best way to keep your mind echoing good vibrations? Give your mind good input material. The greatest limitations, by far, that the mind labors under are the inputs it is subjected to.

The mind is a powerful organ that connects the tangible to the intangible – thoughts to action – but the mind is only as good as what it is exposed to. In computing terms, GIGO (Garbage In Garbage Out), a concept computer programmers are more than familiar with. It means that computers are only as good as what is put into them. If you feed garbage into a computer (input), then you are going to get garbage out (output). The human mind is the same. If you feed it bad inputs, it won't give you the best outputs possible.

This is both the mind's greatest weakness and its greatest strength, depending on the inputs you provide it with. If you expose your mind to superior content and provide your brain with stable nutrition, then you will find you can take advantage of the mind's power. If you provide your brain with high glucose-based energy and expose your mind to poor content, then what you will have is a mind that performs erratically.

You and your mind have different command and control mechanisms. Your mind and brain together have evolved as highly competent command systems that make your body do what the brain commands. But you do not have a solid line of control over the mind. We tell it what to do, and when it compiles – great. But there are many times that it can't comply, doesn't know how to comply, or just simply won't comply. For these times, hacking is the solution.

It all begins by differentiating *you* from *your mind*. (Throughout this book, *you* will always refer to "you," not your mind.)

Activity 2.2: Observe the inputs

As you continue to observe the activities of your mind, observe and evaluate what you are putting into your mind. Your mind is molded by the experiences that you allow it to experience. Evaluate the kinds of entertainment you expose yourself to, the types of books you read, the movies you watch, the ideas you absorb, and the activities you take part in.

Write your observations and evaluations in your journal.

You'll know what to do to improve the inputs you provide your mind, if you think about it – for now, just remember that everything you expose yourself to influences how your mind develops and functions.

Chapter 3: The Mind's Codes

Once you get the hang of watching your mind's activity and observing the kinds of things it looks at, what it worries about, or what it keeps going back to, then you will start to really understand what is happening in your mind. Then, you can get to work hacking your mind to function at optimal levels to do all the things you want it to do.

You need your mind to make things happen in the physical world. Your mind is your tool for interacting with the physical world – in just the same way that your iPhone is your tool for interacting with the online world. Your mind provides you with its ability to interact with and extract benefits and experiences from the physical world. However, your mind does better when it has good direction from you. Without you, your mind is like that thrashing fire hose.

By developing your ability to step away from your mind, observing it separately, you will start to see the mind in its element, its real nature, and how it thrashes around without steady control. Then, by taking a "hacking" approach, looking for ways to work around its natural design, you'll be able to direct your own mind in whatever way you need.

"Buggy" code – how you got it

As you get better and better at stepping back from your mind to see it separately, you will gradually start to notice the codes that tell it to run in particular ways. However, most of the code written into your mind wasn't anything you consciously keyed in on some kind of ethereal keyboard. Most of your code has been written by experiences, culture, and what you have been taught – without you realizing it. But, just like the computer code that tells a computer to beep when a message comes in, codes can be altered to mute the incoming alert or raise its volume.

Your code is written by all the things that happen to you. Early in your life, what happens to you is the result of external influences. Heck, even your existence was not something you or your mind planned. The moment you come into this world, your code starts to be written. More and more code is written through the influence of your family, friends, TV, school, games, activities, social interactions, and anything else you experience. Some of those codes are buggy or conflict with other parts of the code. As you progress, the code becomes more complex, with more data and facts written into your memory. The rate of new code getting written and installed in your mind expands at an exponential rate.

And, finally, here you are. Fully coded, bugs and all.

Why is one man polite and another man is not? Is the rude man "bad" and the polite one "virtuous"? No. Why does one person get anxious before an exam, while their friend does not? Why does one person always choose the healthy meal, while the other binges on junk foods every night? The code that has been written into their brains dictates how they behave, how they think, how they interpret the world.

And if you remain passive, like the computer, more code continues to be written for you, outside of your awareness, by external forces, circumstances, and experiences. And that code will continue to have bugs, inconsistencies, flaws, and conflicts.

When a computer has a "buggy" program, the output has glitches, and sometimes the entire program crashes, and needs a reboot. In humans, that "bugginess" manifests as stress, breakdowns, anger, anxiety, and the general sense of being overwhelmed.

The people and experiences that contributed to your original code have faded into the background, while you are left standing independent with a mash-up of codes that give you conflicting perceptions, information, and feelings. You try to do something about it, but your mind is running on incompatible sets of code, and it won't let you get in and change it. You find yourself achieving less than you want, and what you do is unfulfilling. "Hacking" it is a way for you to work around your mind's limitations, the conflicting codes, and the obstacles it presents to change.

What can be even worse than code that dictates how you behave is code that dictates how you perceive things. That can result in unimaginable suffering. Your life traces an arc based on the decisions you make. You base those decisions on how you perceive the given situation or issue. The trajectory your mind takes from one experience to the next, your life today, and the opportunities that come your way are all rooted in the way you perceive what happens to you.

You need to sit with this idea for a minute. How you experience life is not at all about what happens to you, but about how you perceive what happens to you. That perception occurs in your mind. If you are *in* your mind (*in* the movie as opposed to outside watching it), then you only see what the mind sees, the perception that has been coded into it. If you are *above* your mind, you can see the bigger picture, that your perception of what happens is the result of the codes in your mind, and that, as the director, you can change it, create your own "director's cut."

Debugging the code

As you've seen, the first step to hacking your own mind is to realize that you are not your mind. Your mind, as powerful as it is, just runs the code. To be truly in charge of your own life, to be the director and programmer of your own script, you'll need to rewrite some parts of that code, but before you can do that, you have to take the "bugs" out of that code.

Loops

The mind works and thinks in loops. When those loops are subconscious, you will only see the outcome of the loop. When those loops are conscious, you can see them going around and round. This is like a computer that executes a program, or a section of code, running it in loops.

When my youngest child became interested in computers, he started off with programming microcontrollers. Those are little devices acting as a computer designed to interface with real-world physical objects. His first design was a sensor hooked up to his bedroom door to detect if someone came in. The code that went into programming his microcontroller had just three lines. Those three lines of code told the microcontroller to look for a break in the invisible laser beam that went from one side of the door across to a sensor on the other side. If you put your hand through the beam, it was broken, and the alarm sounded.

How did the code know how to know if something interrupted the beam? It asked. The three lines of code simply kept asking the sensor, "Did it break yet?" If the beam was not broken, the sensor would return a negative. As long as the answer was negative, the alarm would not sound.

That simple question was coded as a loop. Each time the answer was "no," the program would repeat the question until the answer was "yes." Then it would sound the alarm. It was an infinite loop that ran thousands of times per second, faster than you could decipher or interpret it, just keeping on asking the question (like my youngest son on a long road trip asking, "Are we there yet?") over and over.

And that is just how our brain works – in infinite loops, always querying, looking for a break in the chain, or a break in the sequence. Our mind is all about loops. It is an efficient and effective design, but it can also be one of the brain's greatest design flaws – when it works against us. Love it or hate it, it is what we have. The important thing is to figure out how to use it, or work around its limitations, in a word, to "hack" it.

If you still aren't sure what a loop might look like in a concrete sense, remember the last time you weren't able to get a tune out of your head, one that just played over and over. (At this very moment, I can't seem to get a 90's Britney Spears tune out of my head.) A song gets stuck playing in your head in a repetitive loop, sometimes for days. In a more debilitating example, individuals with OCD (Obsessive Compulsive Disorder) exhibit thoughts and behaviors that go in loops.

Our minds run, at the fundamental level, on loops and associations. Associations of the same thought can come around and around repeatedly, and if they are relevant, we pick up on it. It is a brilliant system, but it has flaws if we don't take control of it. Loops are everywhere. Even sleep runs on loops. Babies, for example, go through cycles while they sleep, with their bodies doing a periodic system check for hunger. IF the baby is hungry, THEN it wakes up crying.

Some loops are small and used for inconsequential issues. At other times, small loops connect up to form larger loops, and larger loops combine to become even more complex loops. Those complex loops are responsible for how the mind works. Loops and associations are really the bits and bytes of the human mind. Those loops can produce either good or bad results.

Being successful or unsuccessful, being happy or being broken in life, being ambitious, or being anything else are all kinds of loops.

One typical loop defines the potential your mind believes you have. If you were raised to think you have infinite potential, then, in your mind, you will have a loop that always tells you that you have potential, that you can do anything you want. If, instead, you were raised to think that you are worthless, then that worthless loop will play over and over in your mind, getting in the way of your success. It all comes back to a loop that was programmed into your mind a long time ago. And that is only one small loop.

Your attitude to failure and mistakes can be another small and persistent loop in your mind. If you were taught that mistakes were unacceptable, that'll be a small loop that keeps replaying just under your conscious thoughts. Then, when you make a mistake, you feel like crap. You feel guilt. Guilt leads to frustration. Frustration leads to anger, and as my master, Yoda, would say, "...anger leads to the dark side." Nonetheless, that loop plays continuously in your mind. Whenever you try something that fails, that loop kicks in, and eventually you may stop trying. Thomas Edison, you shall not be. As a variant that avoids making mistakes entirely, you may have a loop that doesn't even allow you to expend the effort unless the outcome is certain, a loop for the unwillingness to take risks.

There's a saying – "success is a habit" – and it's true. Success is a habit made up of loops. Potential is converted into action by attitude. If you don't care about making a mistake – and I don't mean the reckless kind of mistakes – then you can go all out. When you go all out, and you make a mistake, then you can pick yourself up and try again. With each try, you have more data about what doesn't work. But it is the sense of your own potential that allows you to keep banging away at it until you get to where you need to be. That's an attitude loop that encourages you to make an effort, fed by the loop that provides you with the sense of your own potential, and supported by a loop that lets you try again when you make a mistake. When you achieve a successful outcome and are rewarded for it, it creates an altogether new loop – one we describe as a "habit."

Habits

Habits have three component parts: a **trigger**, an **act**, and a **reward**. If you do something a few times when a specific condition is present, and you experience a reward for doing it, the mind starts to see the action as something you should keep doing when the trigger is present. And that's a habit.

We create all sorts of habits – some of them "bad." I have a habit with chocolates. It's a rudimentary habit. I feel down, I eat a chocolate, I feel good. The trigger is I feel down. Instantly, I take a chocolate bar from my laptop bag (I used to keep a ready supply of Mars Bars and Snickers in it). I eat it (the act), and I feel good (the reward).

Eventually, the habit just started running on autopilot, and I would automatically reach inside my bag without even realizing that I was feeling low or hungry. I even directed my assistant to keep my bag constantly supplied with Snickers and Mars Bars. Before I realized it, I had gained 30 lbs.

Habits can keep you doing something until you don't even realize you are doing it – and the next thing you know you've hit 30 lbs., or chewed off all your fingernails, or are up to smoking two packs a day. Habits can also keep you making successful moves – until you have achieved a successful outcome, graduating with a degree, building a business, writing a book, growing a garden.

Habits can be "good" or "bad" or even benign, depending on whether they help you or hinder you in getting what you want.

Habits are constructed from smaller loops nested inside larger loops. Some people reach for chocolate whenever they feel depressed. Depression is, itself, a self-reinforcing loop. When that loop runs, it triggers another loop, and then that triggers a reward that triggers another loop.

Loopy, right?

But this is good. Because we can work with loops. In fact, hacking your mind is all about working with loops. All you need to do is create a new loop for your mind to pick up on and the next thing you know it displaces the old loop. Whether it is eating unhealthy foods, smoking, or some other bad habit, you just need to displace one loop with another loop – and you can change your life. If it's a helpful loop you want to keep or a new one you want to create, you can struggle to complete that loop every time – or you turn that loop into a habit.

That's all attitudes are too – loops that become habits. If you have the right attitude, then you will put in a good measure of effort. When you put in the effort, without distraction, then you will win more than you lose. Winning and succeeding are, in themselves, an intrinsic reward. Suddenly, having the right attitude becomes a habit.

There will be some things that won't pan out the way you expect, but when you habitually put in your best consistent effort, most things you do will work out. When they do work out, you succeed, and you expand your sense of your own potential. With an expanded sense of potential, you'll find yourself having a better attitude, because you succeeded the last time. That, in turn, turns into super effort, and, when that works out too, you have an even better attitude and even greater potential. This is a positive self-reinforcing loop that has become a habit.

On the other hand, if you have a poor attitude, and you go into a situation, thinking, "This is not going to work out," then you are likely to quit before anything comes of it or you won't put in much effort, and you will fail. So, you announce that you knew all along that it was a fool's errand, and your attitude suffers even more. It's a classic downward self-reinforcing loop.

When you look at each of these scenarios, which of the self-reinforcing loops do you find yourself in more often? Do you mostly find yourself in positive loops or negative loops? Whichever you regularly find yourself in, it has probably become a habit.

If you are always operating in a successful loop, then you don't need to do any debugging in that area – unless you want to make it even better. But if the negative loop scenario sounds familiar to you, then you need to pause for a minute, examine the loops you find yourself in, and ask yourself some questions.

Looking at a downward or negative loop that runs in your life, at what point in the loop do you think you can break the downward spiral?

Can you break that spiral at the potential loop, the attitude loop, the effort, or the outcome?

Of course, your ultimate goal is to change the outcome – that's the whole point. But the outcome is not where you can make the change; you need to change something that can lead to the better outcome.

Of course, you also need to have the potential for doing it – but that's not so much about what you have as it is about what you perceive you have. If you believe that you have the potential, then you will have it, but if you believe otherwise, then you won't – it's a loop. In my experience, everyone has potential. When I look at anyone, I see potential, even when they don't see it in themselves. No one has zero potential. They may temporarily lose it, misplace it, or forget how to access it, but everyone has potential.

So, in breaking that downward spiral, that leaves attitude and effort to focus on. You need to be able to put in a wholehearted effort in whatever you are doing and that requires the right attitude. Attitude is in the mind, and, while effort is expressed through the muscles, it begins in the mind. And since attitude and effort are found in the mind, they are hackable, and where you should apply your changes.

How do you get over a habit? You replace it with something else. That is how many people quit smoking. They get a patch. The patch replaces the nicotine while eliminating the physical act of smoking. Once the act of smoking stops, half the battle is won. This is the replacement of one loop with another loop. To get rid of a negative loop, you need to displace it. The best way to debug a bad habit is to replace the loops in the habit with different new loops. The habit is dismantled – one loop at a time.

And remember habits themselves are loops. Change a few of the loops that make up the habit, and the habit will change. Replace any of the loops in the habit, and the habit is disrupted. Better yet, replace all the loops, and you have a brand-new habit.

That is how you debug a habit, and that is essentially how you debug any part of the overall code.

All of code in your mind is made of loops. Change any loop, you change the code. How do you change a habit? You replace it – one loop at a time.

I used to have many addictive habits. I liked having habits, because they provided a sense of predictability. Do this, get that. And I avoided changing any of them, because I used to think that to change a habit you needed tremendous discipline.

Discipline & effort, resonance & momentum

Discipline is really a kind of a loop of its own. **Discipline** can generally be understood as using effort to do something, working against the forces opposing it. Discipline can be the hard way to do things. But it doesn't have to be that way.

When discipline and effort are used to install a new or different loop to replace an old loop that you want to get rid of, it becomes difficult when the new loop is out of sync with the rest of the things going on in your mind and your life. Discipline is often used to force an outcome through effort, working against opposing forces. However, discipline can also be used to work with existing forces to amplify the effort expended.

Imagine trying to punch a large sand-filled punching bag at the gym. Newton's Law of Inertia states that a body at rest tends to stay at rest. Right? So, when you strike that first blow, you're going to move that bag a little in the direction of the punch by the sheer force (effort) of your punch. If, instead, you strike the bag when it is coming toward you, what happens? Or, if you hit the bag on its swing away from you, what happens? Striking the bag on the swing away from you sends it the furthest of all because you are working with and adding to the existing momentum, whereas striking it when it's on its way toward you will injure your wrist because you are working against momentum.

The same goes for discipline. You have to "jujitsu" it around, rather than using blunt force efforts to force something to be the way you think it should be. You should apply your effort when the tide is with you, moving in the direction you want to move, not when the tide is against you.

Resonance occurs when you apply effort or force at the right time, which magnifies the effort. Using discipline to apply force at the wrong time diminishes the effort. But, remember, discipline can also be used to apply the effort when it produces the greatest effect.

As an illustrative example, let's look at my experience with the addictive habit of smoking. I used to smoke two packs a day. The brightest part of my morning was lighting that first cigarette. When my first child was born, I had to cut back, having fewer opportunities to smoke after we turned the house into a no smoking zone. Studies were exposing the dangers of second-hand smoke. Worse, the smell of smoke in the air, on clothes and drapes, predisposes kids to smoke later in life, so we decided to keep the house smoke-free.

I made the effort to get to work earlier just to get my first morning smoke, and I stopped at the gym on my way home from work to shower and change into a fresh set of clothes. This went on for two years.

However, my child was a precocious two-year-old, and one day he asked me, point blank, what the odd "stinky" was that he smelled on me. I had thought I did a good job of getting rid of all the traces of smoke, but a non-smoker can always pick out the smoker because the smell is so strong.

I came clean about my smoking, but my son couldn't understand what it was all about. I didn't want to sing the virtues of smoking to him, so I couldn't say much, but he grabbed hold and wouldn't let the subject go. One day, he found a pack of my cigarettes, and the picture on it horrified him, so he began pestering me to quit. Try explaining the concept of addiction to an almost-three-year-old. You can't.

I felt I had no choice but to quit. And I did it cold turkey. That was the last time I smoked – twenty years ago. I did it the old-fashioned way. I put in all my effort and stoked up the discipline to get the 40 cigarettes a day addiction down to 0 in one afternoon. I sat, that night, at my desk without a box, pack, or any cigarettes in the house. It wasn't bad yet, because I was still at home where there were no triggers, since I hadn't been smoking at home for three years.

But I knew my office was going to be a trigger-rich environment. So, the next morning, I called my assistant and told her to cancel or postpone all my meetings for the next week. I stayed away from the office and had contractors go in and renovate my office. I left instructions for what needed to be done. Then my wife and I packed up our child, and we went on vacation for five days. Drastic? Yes.

But, remember, we talked about triggers, actions, and rewards as the components that form a habit.

Places can be triggers. Events can be another kind of trigger. So, instead of fighting the flow, the momentum of the habit, I stepped away from it and reduced my exposure to the triggers. Then, all I had to contend with was the nicotine withdrawal. (I didn't use nicotine patches.)

To debug my smoking habits, I altered my surroundings, my schedule, and my triggers. In essence, I got around the habit, hacking it, in order to change it. As many as possible of the loops that I had that were associated with smoking were displaced by new loops and new triggers during that week away in the mountains. I ate more, drank more coffee, and just hunkered down – and relied on good old discipline whenever those proved temporarily inadequate.

As my experience with quitting smoking shows, changing loops and habits is a holistic affair. Not only do you need to change the loops themselves, but you need to make those changes in a way that doesn't clash with the established movement and momentum of the things around it.

When you try to energize the swing of a pendulum, you can't do it when it is on its way toward you, that is, when the momentum is against you. You need to wait until the pendulum has begun to swing away from you. Then your effort will be aligned with the pendulum's momentum, and you will achieve what you want.

Otherwise, you just mess up the harmony of the swing.

If you already have an entrenched habit, don't go into battle with it. You want to change your habit, not beat yourself up while you are doing it. The habit is more likely to win a direct battle.

Certainly, if you put enough effort into anything, you will see results, but combine that effort with a hacking approach, and you will see the effort-to-reward ratio tilt in your favor. Successful people know how to do this, even make a habit of it, getting into a loop "on the ground floor," where the momentum is working with them and then just give it 110 percent.

Eliminating unnecessary distractions

An important thing to tackle in debugging the code in your mind is unnecessary distraction. Distractions are both a coding problem, and an obstacle to debugging other parts of the code. Rooting out distractions is an art and takes years of practice. First, we need to define what a distraction is, and then we need to look at the type of distraction.

A distraction is anything that crosses your path that is not immediately necessary for the task at hand. If you are watching a movie, a text from a dear friend, no matter how close, is still a distraction. Calling your mom, while she is grading a student's essay, is a distraction for her, because you aren't part of grading the essay. Some distractions are acceptable, even welcomed. Other distractions are not.

If you're trying to get your taxes done, and it's 30 minutes to midnight, the most delectable ice cream and movie by the fireplace is an unwelcome distraction. Much of the time distractions are appealing, because we want to do the thing that is more fun than what we have to do. Other distractions are annoying, because they interrupt the thing that is more fun or more urgent.

Either way, the clear problem is that, once there is a distraction, our minds are rendered inefficient.

Hang on a sec... my son wants to play chess. Will be right back....

Okay, I'm back. See, some distractions are more pleasurable than others. But they are distractions nonetheless.

So, we need to categorize distractions. Not every distraction needs to be expunged from our life. Some distractions can give us meaning and purpose, or even give us a much-needed boost, so that we can get back to what we were doing before, renewed or better in some way. There are times when the mind is exhausted with what it has been doing, so it seeks out distractions. That allows it to get away from the matter at hand and provides the opportunity for a higher inspiration to work on it in the background.

The distractions we especially want to control are the ones that appear in our mind unbidden and are so engrossing that we forget our intentions. The distraction that takes us away from something we want to accomplish often operates on some kind of loop.

If-Then loops

A person who is easily distracted is typically someone with a faulty If-Then loop. Or probably more than one.

In coding computer programs, one of the most popular kinds of loops is the If-Then loop. An If-Then loop is used when you want the code to do something dependent on something else. The code tells the computer IF this condition is fulfilled, THEN do that action. When you place that in a loop, the loop runs until the condition is satisfied, and then it does the action it is programmed to do.

The brain has its own If-Then loops running for almost everything you are involved in. One simple loop is this: IF energy levels low, THEN feel hungry. Not elegantly stated, but you get the point. Even fear runs on If-Then loops. IF this happens, THEN feel afraid.

For distractions, one of your If-Then loops might be: IF you are feeling frustrated, THEN seek out stimulation elsewhere. Or perhaps the If-Then loop may be: IF a friend calls, THEN drop whatever you are doing. There are thousands of possible variations.

What you need to do is find the IFs and the THENs in your own loops and evaluate whether they are warranted or helpful. You also need to identify the root loop – the fundamental loop. In the next chapter, we'll be talking about how to get to that fundamental loop.

You must do this carefully. If you remove the wrong If-Then pair, the consequences can be catastrophic. You can apply this, for now, to distractions, and even then, be cognizant of what you are doing.

Erasing the "bugs" in your own loops will change the way your mind triggers different cognitive, visceral, and emotional responses. If you are someone who has anxiety issues, then you will find that hacking your loops will make a lot of difference in the way you handle your mind, your body, and life in general. Changing the loops can help with anger issues, procrastination, self-sabotage, fear of speaking, and any of an almost unlimited number of issues.

The one who eliminates the "buggy" loops, by the way, is *you*, not your undirected mind, not some outside force. If you need to erase certain sections of the coding in your mental loops, you do that by displacing them. It is too challenging and limiting to try to eradicate a loop without putting something else in its place. So, replace a faulty loop with a loop that is beneficial.

But just how do you replace a faulty loop? You need to start by identifying what you want to change.

Activity 3: Identify your habits, good & bad

List all the habits you have, as many as you can think of, small and large. At this point, don't worry about whether the habits are bad or good. Just identify as many as you can.

Next, make a separate list of things you think would make your life easier if they were habits.

Go back to your first list, and identify the ones you think are good habits and the ones you think are bad habits. Then write down why you think each one is good or bad.

Chapter 4: Fundamental Loops and Virtual Models

This chapter will give you two important ways to identify and better understand what is going on in your mind, so that you can work with your mind instead of against it. The first is a technique to dig down and discover the root of a loop. The second is to understand the virtual world you have been building in your mind.

To accomplish the first, you will learn a new practice that will help you understand why your mind does the things that it does. This technique is taught in Ivy League business schools but is not always practiced in big companies. The ones who do, though, seem to stay on top.

Activity 4.1: Rooting out the fundamental loop: the "Why?" exercise

This is an easy exercise, designed to get to the root of anything. All you need to do is ask a series of eight questions, and, usually, you will get to the bottom of the matter by the time you get to your eighth answer.

Here are the questions:
1. Why...?
2. Why...?
3. Why...?
4. Why...?
5. Why...?
6. Why...?
7. Why...?
8. Why...?

No, I'm not trying to be funny. Kids do this all the time, but we either take it for granted or get cross with them. Yet, it is the way the mind naturally works, using a loop of asking for a reason and justification for every answer. How else can you get to the bottom of things? Children instinctively have it right. When you apply this strategy to the contents of your own mind and to the things it does, you can slowly start to see the mind's own foolish (or brilliant) ways.

Pick one of the bad habits you identified in the last activity which has been prevalent in your life. Apply this simple procedure of asking "Why?"

repeatedly until you have no place left to go. Here is the way it might go.

1. Why am I always late for work? Because I don't like going to work.

2. Why don't I like going to work? Because I might be criticized by my boss.

3. Why would I be criticized by my boss? Because I doubt that I'm good at my job.

4. Why do I doubt that I'm good at my job? Because I don't think I learned it well.

5. Why do I think I didn't learn my job well? Because I am not a good learner.

6. Why am I not a good learner? I don't know, but my teachers told me I wouldn't amount to anything, because I don't have the ability to learn.

That was done in six questions. Saying that you need to ask eight questions isn't really an accurate statement of what you need to do to get to the bottom of the subject at hand – it's just a convenient estimate. Sometimes, you will be able to do it in six, but, other times, you may need to ask "Why?" many more times.

The point is to go down the rabbit hole that each answer creates. Before long, you will start recognizing and identifying loops that are active in your mind. You will find that some loops are just absurd. Nevertheless, they reside deep within your mind at work in your mental programming.

Virtual models, self & self-image

In this book, we have really been dealing with various forms of the self. The *"I"* directs the mind, while the mind has the responsibility of managing the body and the reality around it.

Many people are entertained by the antics of their own mind. The moment their mind takes off on one of its associative flights of daydreaming, they sit down to watch the movie, relishing whatever the mind has to offer. These mental movies and antics are, in fact, the basis for the great power of prediction that the mind has. That power begins with the mind's ability to create models.

To hack our own minds, we've already been discussing how *you* (the subject) are viewing *your mind* (the object). The object and the subject are two very different things. The object, in philosophy, is the thing being observed. The subject is the one that does the observing. For example, if you are looking at a ball, the ball is the object, and you are the subject.

Now, we need to take that one step further. The mind operates within a neurochemical organ, the brain, and it needs to make a neurochemical replica of whatever it sees, hears, feels, smells, and tastes, in other words, of whatever it observes. To be able to understand how the object works and how it responds, the mind needs to make a virtual replica of the object in the mind.

In the late 20th century, research scientists came up with a new way to test things. Before, when someone wanted to test something, they had to go out and run a test with the real object. For example, they had to build a test plane and actually fly it to understand how it would operate under real world conditions. They still do that, of course, but more selectively and not as often as they once did, because now aerospace engineers also use a method known as *non-destructive testing*. It uses computational models placed into computational environments where a computer calculates and predicts how something will behave in any given situation.

That is essentially the same way that your mind predicts its own encounters with its environment. In your mind, there are different models of objects and environments. Every time you interact with an object, those models are updated to increase the accuracy of future predictions.

Imagine, if you will, taking a drinking glass and dropping it out of a third-floor window. What will happen when it hits the asphalt? Can you imagine the result? Of course, you can. Is the result the same if the glass lands on the grass? If I, now, asked you to imagine dropping an object made of the latest material, Napherene, would you be able to see, in your mind, what happens when the object strikes the asphalt? No. The reason is that you don't know the properties of Napherene. (Napherene doesn't exist.) Because you don't know what Napherene is, it has never been subjected to your senses or your reasoning faculties, and so you have no model of it in your mind, and you don't know how it will behave in the environmental model in your mind.

We spend our entire lives building up intricate models of environments, objects, incidents, people we know, events, ideas, and everything else we experience. Brand management is an entire field built around this idea. A brand, logo, trademark, color, jingle, or buzzword are designed specifically to evoke a model in our mind of an experience of a product, place, or promise. That model gives us the sense that we can predictably know what will happen (with the product, place, or promise) as we interact with it in our mind's mockup.

There is one more element in our mental mockup that we haven't yet talked about, and that is the model of our own self. In our mind, we have a version of our self, of who we think we are. This is what we can call the "ego." To get a better result from hacking the mind, we need to take a closer look at the ego in this virtual environment.

Although we often refer to someone who has an over-inflated view of themselves as having an "ego," everyone has an ego. For this book, don't confuse the ego with something that makes you act obnoxious, with being conceited or "egotistical." The ego we are talking about is not an ego that is over-inflated or thinks too highly of itself.

For our purposes, the ego can be understood as a software version of the person. It is a replica created in the mind to model its own interactions with the world to have better experiences or better outcomes. But a lot of problems can arise with this. When the replica is not consistent with the real-world manifestation, conflicts can occur. Imagine what could happen if your virtual replica, your ego, is able to bench press 300 pounds, but your real self is only able to bench press 80 pounds.

Think back to that model of the glass falling from the third floor as you imagined dropping it. Who, in your imagination, is it that does the dropping? Who holds the glass out the window? The mind needs a model for the actor in that scenario. A sane person would visualize themselves as themselves instead of visualizing themselves as Arnold Schwarzenegger. Such a discrepancy could cause some real real-world problems.

So, just how close does the virtual model come to the real thing? The model that you make up in the virtual world impacts your real-world life in two ways. Either it can help you to create outcomes that are exactly the way you intend them, or it can have you living in an "alternative reality."

Imagine that you have a completely unrealistic model of yourself in your virtual world, and you encounter a situation where you think you can do something that you can't. Suppose that your ego has been built up to believe that it can swim the English Channel, from Calais in France to Dover in England, and you jump in to swim the English Channel, but your body doesn't know how to swim. What happens? This extreme example demonstrates how the virtual self in your mind can be inconsistent with your real self in the physical world. However, that inconsistency can work in the opposite direction too. Sometimes your virtual self (your self-image!) is incapable of doing something that your real-world self would be perfectly able to do, if only given the chance.

Another version of the problem can arise if you have an inaccurate view of the environment you are in, while your virtual self is accurate. Imagine that you are on the moon but don't know that the moon has less gravity than earth. Based on earth "data," you believe that you need to apply a certain amount of force to jump two feet. But when you act on that model, your jump propels you much higher than you expected, because the environment on the moon does not have the same gravitational pull, and that was not part of the model you were acting from.

The point is that there are two worlds – both are equally real. One is the realm of physical reality. The other is a virtual reality in the mental realm. You can stand back from this virtual reality, stepping in and out of it to see things from different perspectives.

Another way to get a better understanding of this concept of a virtual model of a person's self is to think about a narcissist. A narcissist is a person who has a wildly exaggerated view of himself in his mind's virtual world. Unfortunately, as things grow increasingly inconsistent between how he sees himself and the realities of his actual self and the world and its reactions to him, there is a disconnect that causes damage to his ego. Instead of correcting his virtual self, the narcissist uses others to validate his inaccurate view of himself. To get that validation, he masters the art of manipulation, so that he can get what he is looking for, validation of the virtual self that exists only in his own mind. In other words, the narcissist tries to force reality to conform to the virtual version in his mind, instead of revising the faulty virtual self-image.

Unlike the narcissist, when you understand how you interface with the world around you, you can start to make improvements or adjustments to your own virtual world and to your self-image.

The more you experience the world around you, the better you can predict outcomes, because your virtual world gets closer to the truth of the physical world. You can "hack" your mind by starting to pay attention to the things around you, so that you make better models in your mind. Those better models will, in time, allow you to make better predictions about what you can do in this world, and increase your contribution. That will increase your happiness, and who knows, that may even increase your wealth and stature as well.

There is a strategy that has been advocated across the motivational genre which is to pretend to be who you are not (yet) in order to become that person. You hear it in advice like, "Dress for the job you want, instead of the job you have." If you can control how far you take it when you follow this kind of approach, then it can work fantastically. But the key is not to deviate so far from reality that it starts working against you. At its worst, it can even start becoming an unhealthy delusion.

If you are a senior executive at an investment bank, it's okay to dress up like a CEO. But if you are working in the mail room, dressing like the CEO could be problematic. The distance between the model you create of yourself and how you need to be in "reality" should be closely managed. This strategy is not about having good feelings from pretending to be someone you aren't, but it is about getting into the frame of mind where it is possible to become the new person you want to be. It's about opportunities for growth.

If you keep the gap between reality and your virtual world tight, then you can reap the benefits of having a useful model to work with. But if the gap is too big, then the conflicts between the code and reality will work against you and what you want to achieve.

Activity 4.2: Journal the gap between virtual and actual

Do these two writing exercises in your journal.

1. List times that you expected you would react to something in a particular way but didn't.

Pick one and use the "Why?" question technique until you uncover the fundamental loop that caused the discrepancy between the way you expected to react and the way you actually reacted.

2. Describe your virtual self in detail, not based on "real" evidence, but based on how you see yourself. Describe the traits, ideals, beliefs, and values that you believe you have.

Compare that virtual "you" with your actions in the "real" world.

For example, perhaps you consider yourself an environmentalist who wants to preserve the rain forest because you believe climate change is a real danger. Do your actions rise to the occasion? I firmly believed that I was a proponent of the environment, and I believed the science behind it. But I was caught off guard when I audited my own virtual self against my reality self. I started to notice that my actions (the ones that benefited the environment) weren't voluntary, and other possible actions that weren't compelled were not done. That was a wake-up call for me.

Do you have any areas of your life where you think of yourself in a certain way, but you are not acting in a way that is consistent with that self-image?

Chapter 5: Beyond the Cognitive

Your mind is extremely powerful, capable of running many different loops and nested loops (loops inside loops) in every kind of situation. But that's just talking about cognition, the brain, and how the brain controls the physical body. You have capacities, however, that go beyond the sensory-based cognitive capabilities of the mind. We all have them, but not all of us use them.

The difference between the normal cognitive abilities of the mind and the extrasensory "psychic" capabilities boils down to the ability to concentrate in different modes. And guess what? Concentration is really just another loop.

First, though, understand that concentration is something very different from meditation, although many people confuse them because they can feel like the same thing. Let's talk about why that is.

Think back to the beginning when we talked about separating out the *you* from *your mind*. When you do that, it's like watching a movie from the outside, but when you are stuck in the workings of your mind, it is like being in the movie. Imagine being Tom Cruise and watching the final edited version of *Mission Impossible*. He acted in the movie, experiencing it from the perspective of being inside it, and then he is watching it, as a spectator, from outside of the movie. Get it?

When you step back from your mind, you can still see it doing its thing, thinking, cogitating, raising random thoughts. *You* can observe it. But you are not *in* it. So, when you can observe it, you can also stop observing it. But your mind doesn't stop performing its functions when you stop observing it. It continues to do its tasks. But you have stepped back and stopped observing it.

What do you get at that point?

Silence. You get complete and total silence. The cognitive ability of your brain is still going in full swing, but it is silent as far as you are concerned.

By contrast, meditation changes the frequency of your mind's activity to the point where the thoughts your mind generates and its cognitive abilities are completely slowed down, so that what you are able to see is a relative silence. Meditation literally changes the physical functioning of the brain itself.

That is why meditation and stepping back from your mind can feel the same, even though they are not. One creates a relative silence while the other creates silence. In time, you should be able to do both, but, for now, what you need to do is to simply step back, separating yourself from your mind.

As we have already talked about, all the "hacking" of the cognitive mind that you need to do can be done from that vantage point. As you step back, you can make the various changes to the loops you want to alter. But that just addresses the cognitive abilities of the mind. The loops, habits, and associations are all tools of the cognitive mind.

However, there is a part of you that can be more than cognitive. It is something that all of us have, but distractions tend to block us from being able to access it. That is the part that you can access when you learn to step back from the mind and concentrate in such a way that you no longer hear it, and you discover silence.

The "extrasensory" you

When we talk about being "psychic," we are talking about getting input from outside of the five senses that we are normally consciously aware of. Sight, sound, taste, touch, and smell are all dimensions that you can attach to the memory of a specific object or experience to give you a sense experience profile of it. That is the realm of your mind's cognitive ability.

When you look at a plate of buffalo wings, fresh out of the kitchen, you can smell it, see it, feel it, taste it, and perhaps even hear the sizzle. The profile you get from the plate of hot buffalo wings comes from five senses. That is a cognitive experience of the buffalo wings.

However, information that hasn't come from normal sensory experience, those five senses, is referred to as "extrasensory," and usually assigned to the realm of the "psychic."

Extrasensory abilities rest with *you*, as opposed to the cognitive abilities that rest with your *mind*. We all have those extrasensory abilities, but we don't always know that they are there, and we don't know how to access them. That kind of "psychic" ability is the mirror image of cognitive ability. It is what inspiration, imagination, and connecting with the universe and powers greater than ourselves is made of. That is why, if you try to analyze it with cognitive tools, you can't. Yet, we all know there is more to our "self" than a cognition machine.

Any inventor or forward thinker – like Edison, Einstein, Newton, Steve Jobs – has mastered the ability to go beyond mere sensory perception, reaching into the extrasensory to see what others do not. Einstein's math wasn't as good as you might expect. That's not where he excelled. He was an average mathematician, but Einstein had insight into the universe that was more than what the cognitive brain is capable of. Einstein is considered a genius because he could ask a question in his cognitive mind, and get inspired answers. None of that is simple cognition. That is inspiration. That is a "psychic" ability.

You, too, have extrasensory abilities, but to tap into them, you need to be able to fully separate yourself from your mind, not only to observe it, but also to silence it.

So, it is part silencing the mind, and it is part separating your mind from *you*. There is no suggestion that Einstein was doing something like this consciously. However, it seems likely that it would happen when he was intensely concentrating. And that provides a clue into the nature of the abilities that we are calling "psychic." They require you to hold your concentration and separate your mind from yourself, while keeping your mind quiet at the same time – which allows you to access what is outside normal sense experience, the extrasensory.

Activity 5.1: Breathe into Focus

This activity is a simple one, a focused breathing exercise. All you need to do is breathe naturally and focus on observing your breathing.

Use your breathing to create a rhythm and point of focus for your mind. You are developing a habit for your mind. A loop. Get your mind to focus on your breathing without controlling that breathing. Let your body breathe at its own pace. You are just an observer.

This exercise will help you to develop focus and concentration.

Hacking for "psychic" powers

Most people believe in one way or another that there is more to the life than what we can perceive through our five senses. What we are calling the "psychic" you is the part of you that can perceive what the senses cannot. When you start tapping into the extrasensory dimensions of your mind, your insight into things increases exponentially.

Since the goal is to hack the mind, you will also want to be able to hack the extrasensory dimensions of the mind, so that its powers can also be brought to bear on the universe around you. Fundamentally, the qualities of the "psychic" mind are all about the speed and concentration of the mind, and the extent of the mind's development.

When I was a kid, my dad could tell when I was about to do something that wasn't allowed. I could have sworn that he could read my mind. Then I found that my mom was even better at reading my mind. I found that my grandparents and all the other elders were "psychic" too. It was super weird.

But as I grew up, I started to notice that I, too, began to develop those "psychic" powers until I was able to look at my daughter and see the ideas rolling around her head. I knew my daughter so well that I could just look at her face or the gait of her walk and tell how she was feeling, what she was thinking, or what she was about to do.

Super weird, right?

It was then that I realized that it wasn't that my parents or family were witches or anything like that. They could tell what I was thinking, simply because they understood the way the mind works, and combining that with my character, they knew what the outcome would be. It's like watching a movie and knowing what the ending will be half way into watching it.

This is indeed a super-natural ability. When you get to a point in your life that you have practiced concentration and you have created enough associations in your mind, you begin to see patterns.

Life is all about patterns. Have you noticed how the same things keep happening in your life in similar ways over the course of time? There are patterns and loops in the grand scheme of things and it works out that we always come back around with a second chance to do various things.

It's not that you get a second chances at things like a first marriage or the way you interacted with your parents (those are time-stamped and specific), but the skills you learn and the ways you can use those skills keep coming back around in your life. The faster you learn them, the quicker they can be used to move on to the next level.

If, on the other hand, you keep making the same mistakes every time an issue comes up, you can start descending deeper into chaos and difficulty until you learn what you need to change that pattern. It's like a video game. If you don't get the firing sequence just right, or you don't get the clues right, you get busted back down to the current level.

In the same way, you learn more, and the brain gathers more information, taking in more than you can consciously realize. The more you absorb, the more your insight grows – at an exponential rate. It's not just about data points. It's about constructing your virtual world so well that, eventually, you will be able to accurately predict what happens as a result of the actions you take.

Remember we talked about the virtual models of world and the self. Your mind can become so proficient at creating a virtual world modeled on the physical world that the more data you absorb, the more you can game out scenarios deep into the future and get predictable results.

And that power of prediction is "psychic" if you ask me.

So, just how do you develop that kind of "psychic" mind that can see into the future?

There are four things that you can do to start developing the beyond-cognitive powers of your mind.

#1: Write it down

Writing things down has the unusual capacity to affect the way you process the ideas and information that you write down. Part of it, of course, is simply the focus required to write down a coherent thought compared to the fleeting quality of a thought passing freely through your mental landscape.

When you write stuff down constantly and consistently, it materializes. Write down the things that you want to achieve. Your mind will start to notice the things that it needs to get you to that point.

#2: Talk less

The easiest mind hack that few ever mention is simply to stop talking. Talking less is not just about keeping quiet, it is also about not thinking about what to say next.

When you speak less, the mind conserves resources, not just in the effort it takes to talk, but also in the resources it takes to think. Have you heard that when a person loses one of his five senses the other four are heightened? It isn't that the remaining senses are intentionally heightened, it's that there are fewer input streams to contend with.

The brain is constantly receiving data from the five senses. Visual data goes to the visual cortex, sound from the ears goes to the auditory cortex, smell, touch, and taste all go to their respective cortices. Once interpreted, the data is sent on to the hippocampus for evaluation and memory formation. All that mental activity consumes a tremendous amount of resources. If you want to hack your brain, the best state to be in is a silent one.

#3: Concentrate & pay attention

Concentrating and paying attention is different from observing. Paying attention is about concentrating. We seem to concentrate a lot less these days, since we have data streams from everywhere chiming away in our pockets. Paying attention is taking one stream of input and not allowing yourself to be distracted from it. If you are in a meeting, turn off your phone, and politely ask that the other person does the same. Keep your time precious. Don't allow someone else to waste your time while you sit and idly wait while they spend half their focus with someone on the phone.

In everything you do, do only that. Break any habit of doing more than one thing at a time. Concentration, when it becomes a habit, gives you the power to look deeply into things, so that you will be able to use the increased ability of your mind to predict correctly, to have foresight.

The best way to concentrate is to pull your mind away from things that are intellectually stimulating and allow it to focus on what it is doing in the moment. If you are reflecting, then don't do anything else. If you are reading, stay within the four corners of the document. If you are playing, immerse yourself in the game. This is an old strategy, but it works very well when you are working to build up your concentration muscles.

When you make concentration a habit, you create a loop that goes something like this: Concentrate. IF concentration is broken, THEN discard distraction and return to concentration. Keep that loop running in your head, so that the loop automatically returns you to concentration each time you break concentration for a distraction. In essence, it's a loop designed to snap yourself out of it every time you distract yourself.

#4: Wake up before 5 a.m.

Waking up early is one of the most common habits that successful people have. If you are sleeping late because you are burning the candle on both ends, then you are damaging your health. Otherwise, you are simply missing out on the power of the morning.

Getting up before everyone else and having the time to silently get to all the things you need to focus on allows for 110 percent effectiveness. It sets the tone for the rest of the day. It's like getting a morning workout. Your body's metabolism peaks and stays high for the rest of the day. In the same way, your mind gets going and doesn't stop for anyone.

Early morning is the best time of the day for the highest intensity of thinking. Your mind is clear because it has rested, your subconscious has had time to chew on your queries, and you are full of answers and ideas at this time. The successful person is one that is filled with ideas and the energy to advance those ideas. To hack your mind, it requires the kind of clarity you can get when you wake up before 5 a.m.

Activity 5.2: Concentration exercises

Concentration exercises will help take your ability to extinguish distractions to a new level. The more you push the envelope when it comes to concentration, the more you will be able to see "behind the veil" of anything that is not readily identified or detected by the senses in the present moment of time.

#1: Observe and remember

You can do this exercise wherever you are if you are sitting still. Let's say you are on the train to work. Observe your surroundings without any thought in your head. Do not comment to yourself, judge, or get caught up with the thoughts in your head. Simply concentrate on observing everything that you can.

Then, later, in the evening, take out your journal, and write down everything you can remember.

#2: Listen

Listen to a piece of classical music and try to identify all the instruments being played.

Or sit quietly in the park or at home and listen to the sounds in the distance. Don't pay attention to the sounds around you or in the room. Ignore nearby sounds and noises and listen only for the sounds coming from a distance, locking onto them for as long as you can.

#3: Memorize

The next time someone gives you their phone number, take a good look at it, and try to memorize it.

#4: Notice distractions

As you read the remainder of this book, write a "+1" and the page number in your journal each time you lose your concentration. By writing it down in your journal, you are forced to notice and keep track of how often you are distracted. Over time, with practice, you should notice that you are becoming distracted less often.

Chapter 6: Blueprinting Your Mind

Hacking your mind, like hacking a computer, takes coding, practice, the power of observation, and something else....

Every hacker worth his salt starts off with a plan, a flowchart. If you think of hackers as guys in hoodies in a basement, banging away on computer keyboards backlit in red, think again. Some of the most sophisticated hackers sit in brightly lit buildings, attend strategy meetings with tier bosses, and work with flowcharts that resemble flowcharts for a manufacturing process. The hacking process is structured and meticulous.

Like a hacking campaign, to hack your mind, you need to start with a blueprint of what you want and how you are going to go about getting it. When you hack your mind, you need to have a clear purpose.

Activity 6.1: Journaling for a purpose

Get your journal out and write down all the possible reasons you can think of for wanting to hack your mind. No one else is going to see this journal, so feel free to pour your heart out in point form and get to the root of your purpose. This is your first step. We all have different reasons. From those reasons arise the strategy.

1. Why do you want to hack your mind?

2. What do you think it will do for you?

3. What level of achievement do you want to reach once you have hacked your mind?

Once you get to the root of your purpose, then you have clues to what is missing.

Next, ask yourself, "What is the greatest drain of mental resources that you are facing right now?" Is it financial? Is it family?

What is the greatest thing that, if removed, would allow you to focus at 100 percent?

What is stopping you and what might trip you up as you move forward?

Of course, you are hacking your mind to have a better life. You are hacking your mind so that you can leap ahead and make all those buckets of potential materialize and start paying off.

The journal is a way to create a blueprint of your mind. You can't really hack your mind effectively until you get all your thoughts laid out so that you can understand what your mind has been doing. You need to see the script of the movie.

Conflicting directions

I recently spoke with a talented artist who had been holding off on selling any of her paintings. I asked her what her goals were when it came to her art pieces. Her initial response was that she wanted to be recognized for her work at some point in the future. Fair enough, we all want to be recognized, not for the glamor and fame, but because being valued and appreciated is one way to gauge our contributions in the world.

My next question was to ask her to put a dollar value on her art. Without hesitation, she said, "A million." I admired the confidence and the goal. But, as soon as she said that, one of her conflicting loops kicked in, and instantly, without missing a beat, she said, "I know, that's too high. I guess I could settle for 10 grand."

There were obviously two separate loops running, one of wanting to strive to have a high level of acceptance and appreciation for her work, and another pulling in the opposite direction that it was unacceptable to set her aim so high.

We all do that. There is one side of us that wants to succeed, and there is another side that is unsure of our abilities. Until we resolve that conflict, we are just going to spin our proverbial wheels while we languish in indecision. Within our mind, the two loops are running against each other like a four-wheel drive vehicle with the front wheels spinning forward at full speed, while the rear wheels head backward at full speed. Although it may be producing a lot of smoke, that vehicle is going nowhere fast.

As you "blueprint" your mind, you will start to see where the inconsistencies are, where inaccurate assumptions, distractions, influences, and misunderstandings have become part of your mental coding and have created the incoherence that holds you back. When you take the time and devote the attention to lay it all out in your journal, you will gradually begin to clear those up.

As you lay out what is in your mind, you will start to see that your mind has just been doing what it knows how to do. Your mind is a function of its temporal, spatial, and social environment. What you have put into it, what has been put in for you, and what has simply accumulated has molded your mind into what it is. The functioning of your mind has been shaped through associations, loops, and habits.

While you are blueprinting and inventorying the contents of your mind, remember not to judge yourself or beat yourself up over what you may find. You are not a bad person. At worst, all of us are confused on many different levels. Often the original intention was good, but the consequences become undesirable, especially when conflicts between accumulated codes starts to occur. You have probably heard the saying, "The road to hell is paved with good intentions." That certainly applies here to the years of mental content that has built up in your mind. That is why you need to take the time to lay it all out and look for the inconsistencies and bugs that make your mind – and life – crash.

Just know that you cannot achieve this overnight. It takes time to journal and ferret out the bugs. But what will surprise you is that once you decide to clean up the inconsistencies, and you start journaling, you will see things more and more clearly.

Blueprinting removes the blinders, fallacies, and inconsistencies in your beliefs and automatic assumptions, giving you the opportunity to choose one path or the other. The point is not what path you chose but that you chose one. When you have a purpose, then your "hacking" becomes more useful. If you don't know the direction you intend to go, then you have no way of knowing what to correct, or worse....

Some time ago, a major airliner crash killed hundreds. The accident investigation eventually determined that there was a design flaw in the fly-by-wire system. Fly-by-wire was a new development in flying technology where the pilot's inputs were interpreted by the computer, and then the computer would send the signal to the servos to the control surfaces (ailerons, rudder, elevator and such) to get them to move the amount needed to execute the pilot's intent. If a pilot wanted to bank left, he would shift the joystick in the cockpit left, and the computer would sense that and adjust the ailerons as necessary to execute the bank.

That crash was inexplicable because the pilot had flown straight into an obstruction. It turned out that, while the captain was banking left, the co-pilot was trying to bank right. The computer read both signals and they had canceled each other out. The plane didn't alter direction and slammed into the obstruction straight ahead.

When you don't sort out which beliefs or values you hold, or whether your beliefs and actions are consistent, you will find yourself on a path that does not take you anywhere. You need to pick a direction. Bank left, or bank right. Trying to do both will drive you straight into the side of the mountain.

Doing the "Why?" exercise, found earlier in the book, will help you work your way through all the different sorts of loops in your mind – loops of actions, loops of values, beliefs, and interpretations. It will help you to identify just where your mental programming has inconsistencies and discrepancies.

Hacking your mind isn't about turning yourself into some sort of superhuman. It's really about shedding inconsistencies and discrepancies so that you can pick a course and concentrate on all the things you need to do to reach your goals. It's about identifying conflicts in the code, so that your mind can keep you flying in the direction you want to go, instead of crashing.

You will find that distractions provide some of the biggest conflicts in your mental code. You want to do one thing, move in one direction, but a distraction has you paying attention to something else, steering you in a different direction. Distractions come in all shapes, sizes, and forms, whether it is a movie in the mind, a compelling news story on the TV, or friends who keep posting cute puppy pictures on your social feed. You need to step away from distractions, one and all.

Whether it's an addiction to a substance, an addiction to a television series, or simply an addiction to distractions, you need to remove those vicious loops, but you can't remove them until you uncover them through your journaling. Once you do identify them, you can work your way down to the fundamental (root) loops, and then displace them one at a time.

Once you have done that, the blueprint process is easy. As you are creating your blueprint, remember that *you* are not the same as *your mind*. You are the subject who is looking at your mind. Your mind is your cognitive ability, and your "psychic" mind is the part of you that is adept in the virtual world – the part that gives you insight into the future.

When a successful person looks at an endeavor, they can foresee what will work and what won't.

For example, someone like Warren Buffet can anticipate the future of an investment. His faculties are so highly tuned that he knows exactly what an investment is going to do; when he picks out the features of an investment opportunity and puts them into his finely tuned virtual world, he can anticipate what it's going to do without doubt and hesitation.

To be able to foretell the future, your virtual world and your virtual you needs to be as close to reality as possible. If you don't like what you see, then go out and change that in the real world, and then update the virtual you. Doing it the other way is possible, but it is always better to simulate it inside, but work it in the real outside.

One of the most credible ways to move the mind in the direction you want is to change your action. The change in that action instantly produces results, and those results are experienced as a reward. Pretty soon the act becomes a habit.

Blueprinting a new habit

One of the most important tools in the blueprinting process is to establish clear actions and clear rewards. Say, for instance, you want to start a new habit of exercising every morning at 5 a.m. You need three things, a trigger, an act, and a reward. When you have all three in place, and you have repeated the loop few times, it will become a habit that you will no longer need to compel.

So, in this example, if you want to create a habit of doing a routine morning workout, place a trigger in your room – your gym clothes, perhaps. So, the moment you wake up, you see it sitting on the chair. Pick it up, get changed, and get to your workout. As soon as you are done, give yourself a reward, something you really like – something that you do not always have or that you don't normally consider – perhaps a milkshake, or a delectable slice of fruitcake. It doesn't matter if it cancels out the calories you burned during the workout. Your real objective is not the calories, it's establishing the habit.

When you have rewarded yourself, and your mind has locked onto the habit, then you can stop the treats. By the time your mind realizes that the sweets are no longer forthcoming, it has already started to experience a different sort of reward, the reward of better energy and feeling better from the morning workouts, so the sweets will no longer matter. Now you've created a new loop in your blueprint.

Activity 6.2: Journal for supporting values

Writing in your journal, list the values you hold.

Look for loops that express those values or that hold a value in place and write those down.

If you are having difficulty, use the "Why?" question technique to dig down into your value system.

With that done, identify and make a list of goals that you want to achieve.

Tackling one goal at a time, identify and list the values you hold that promote the achievement of the goal and the values that prevent it.

Decide whether the values that oppose your goal are worth keeping. If they are not, create some new loops to replace the ones you no longer want to keep.

When you finish one working with the values for one goal, move on the next.

* * *

As you start to lay bare the workings of your mind in your journal, remember that it is always going to be a work-in-progress. There will always be changes, new realizations will pop up, new habits will form, new situations will arise, and so on. So, keep your journal vibrant and dynamic. You are never the same person two days in a row. As Heraclitus said, "A man never steps into the same river twice; the river is never the same, and neither is the man." So, keep updating it, and keep referencing it.

Chapter 7: The Body's Contribution to the Mind

Now we come to the body. Just as there are representatives who sit in the U.S. House of Representatives to make the needs of the American people known, the body has representatives in the brain to make its needs known to the rest of the mind. The primal parts of the brain, in particular, are designed to look after many of the body's needs.

In many programs of advancement, we are told to disregard the needs of the body and advance the needs of the mind. Many religious practices and theologies teach that the body is sinful and the soul is to be prioritized. But hacking the mind is really about making sure that there is harmony between the mind, body, and the spirit, so that all parts have the opportunity to reach their full potentials.

The advancement of one does not have to be to the detriment of the others. There is a way to build them all up without taking a zero-sum game perspective. In fact, an optimally functioning and healthy body can help to build the mind and spirit. A powerful mind can help to build and mend the body and advance the spirit. There is a powerful feedback loop connecting body, mind, and spirit. Working together, they all play a role in fulfilling your needs and goals.

For the body to be an active part of the mind's game, the body needs to be as vibrant and healthy as possible.

The body's economy of effort and energy

The body (via the primal parts of the brain) is a highly experienced economist. The body's only currency or resource is energy.

Effort is the ability and intention to overcome hesitation. A body at rest tends to stay at rest, as Newton said. To move that body, energy is required. That energy is a scarce resource. The reward sought for using that energy is more energy. So, if you expend the effort, the body looks to get back more energy than what has been used.

For example, suppose that there is a store a mile away. You need to walk there, and it will take you 1,000 calories to do it. Your mind knows this (or thinks it does) in its virtual platform. But it also knows that there is free food there (or something else that will make it worthwhile). It realizes that, when it gets there, 1,200 calories will be waiting for it. Do you think the body will be motivated to get here? Yes, of course.

The body (or, rather, its representative in the brain) finds the answer to this "problem" by considering three areas:

1. How accurate has the mind's virtual world been in the past about these kinds of things?

2. How many calories are waiting versus how many calories need to be expended?

3. What is the opportunity cost of not doing anything?

If this sounds like a class in Economics 101, it is – it is just an economics of the body, and the mind has mastered it over time, as long as your virtual world is accurate – and that depends on you.

If you have been completely accurate in your assessments of efforts and payoffs in the past, then, when you consider making one of these trips, the body is going to weigh your analysis of the matter and score your endeavor. If it thinks that you have been 100 percent correct in the past, then it will award you a 100 percent weight to the first question of predictability and history. If you have been poor at predicting these things, then you get maybe 50 percent.

Now you go to the next question and look at the calories that need to be expended versus how many stand to be gained.

So, instead, let's say you get 50 percent for the first question. It takes you 1,000 calories of effort and there are 2,000 calories waiting. That means that at 50 percent of 2,000 calories, there are only 1,000 calories waiting for you, and you need to spend 1,000 calories, so the body determines that the benefit is a wash.

After that, the qualitative question of opportunity costs is factored in. This can take into account a broad range of other things, such as the opportunity to meet up with friends or the chance just to get out of the house.

Then, the body makes the decision. If the decision is to go, then you feel enthusiastic and motivated. If the decision is not to go, then the body feels lazy and hesitant.

This applies to every situation. There is always an economic analysis at the bottom of it. What the mind can control are the factor inputs. If you have been accurate in your analysis in the past, then your body is more certain of what is to come. If you have been prone to exaggeration, the body will take that into consideration. It's always good to not exaggerate.

But now, let's say *you* really want to go, even though the body is feeling lazy. That's where you'll need to hack your mind so that it can get the body to do what *you* want, to go to the place where the reward is waiting.

Whenever you feel lazy about doing something, realize that your body hasn't calculated the payoff in the way you do, and you will need your mind to pull the levers to make it happen. In most cases, the mind will take the side of the body, so you'll need to hack the mind to make the body do what you want.

When you want your body to do something, you to have to play a long-term game with it. You have to make sure that you never complain about the things you initiate, and, more importantly, you have to make a habit of being grateful and thankful for the things that you get. This will convey the message to the body that what you want it to do are things that it should be enthusiastic about doing.

Activity 7: Gratitude hack

In your journal, review all the loops you have identified, and, instead of criticizing the bad loops that you believe are ruining your life, praise the good loops. Leave the bad ones alone, and, instead, be grateful for the loops that make you do well. You can displace the bad loops later.

This activity is about hacking your brain with praise and thanksgiving. Praise your positives and be grateful that you have them. It's like getting a child to do well in school. If you praise the child for all the things they do right, you will find that they do right more often, and for self-motivated reasons instead of having to be bribed to do something.

Chapter 8: Hacking the Tangible Brain

How you move, how you eat, what you eat, and a whole host of things affect the physicality of the brain, and all of that has an impact on the effective functioning of the mind. Understanding how the physical brain and body affects your mental functioning will help you hack your brain to bring your mind to a new level of effectiveness. And the healthier your physical brain is, the more impact all your other mind hacking efforts will have.

It is common to talk about the brain and the mind as if they were the same thing, confusing them. They are, however, two separate things. The brain is what you find when you look inside the cranial vault. It has mass, shape, volume, weight, and all the other things that trigger sensory perceptions. In other words, it is tangible.

The mind, on the other hand, is not something you can pick up, slice open, look into, or otherwise handle in any interactive sort of way. The mind is intangible. However, the mind's intangibility does not make it any less real than the brain. Both are equally real, but different manifestations of existence. One is tangible like a pebble on the beach; the other is intangible like the force of gravity.

This universe is composed of two balancing phenomenon - all things are either tangible or intangible, and they always exist in pairs, like the brain and the mind. Planets around the sun are tangible, for instance, but the dark matter and space between those celestial bodies is intangible. Throughout nature, this balance between tangible and intangible is inextricable – when one exists, the other is there as well – you just have to find it. They are not opposites; they are symbiotic. A living person is made up of a tangible body and an intangible life. Without the intangible, the body is lifeless.

This is also true of the human brain and mind. The brain provides the structural and physical presence – the tangible side of the story of human cognition – while the mind is the intangible side.

A lot of what you want to do and who you want to become depends on your brain. In that balancing of the tangible and intangible, to have your mind functioning at its best also requires that you make sure your physical brain is functioning at its best.

So, let's turn our attention to the physical qualities of the brain.

The brain

The brain is just three pounds of gray and white matter. The gray matter consists of neurons and is about 40 percent of the brain, while the other 60 percent is white matter, consisting of dendrites and axons, which are responsible for the transmission of data. The brain has the consistency of a wet custard and is 60 percent fat by volume and 75 percent water by weight.

The brain can consume as much energy as a 20-watt light bulb and uses 20 percent of the blood flow in a person's body. All those resources reach the brain via a vast and intricate web of blood vessels. There are approximately 100,000 miles of blood vessels involved in the supply and return of blood to and from the brain. The brain is a resource hog, consuming more resources than any other organ of the body.

The brain has three functional areas, the cerebrum, cerebellum, and the brain stem. The **cerebrum** is the largest and is further divided into four lobes, the frontal, parietal, temporal, and occipital lobes. The **frontal lobe** is responsible for a vast array of human thought and action. It plays a major part in motor function, memory, judgment, and impulse control. It is also responsible for social and sexual behavior. The **parietal lobe** is where sensory information like taste, touch, and pressure is processed. The **temporal lobe** holds the areas of language comprehension, hearing, long-term memory, and the ability to recognize faces. Finally, the **occipital lobe** is involved with the interpretation of visual stimuli.

The **cerbellum**, located at the back of the head below the cerebrum, is responsible for movement, position, and coordination.

The **brain stem** is the most primitive part of the brain, responsible for the maintenance of automatic survival functions, such as breathing, heart beats, and more.

There is, of course, much more to the brain. The lore that we use less than 10 percent of our brains is patently false. We know varying amounts about specific areas of the brain, but, for the most part, science still has a long way to go in objectively mapping our brain and understanding how it behaves.

For now, here are a few of the major areas of the physical brain.

Cerebral Cortex. This part of the brain is where conscious thought and intelligence is processed. It is instrumental in our ability to remember, pay attention, and remain self-aware. It is the outer layer of the cerebrum and is made up of folded gray matter.

Corpus Callosum. The two cerebral hemispheres of the cerebrum are connected by one bridge that allows data to flow between the two. This is the corpus callosum.

Ventricles. Four pockets filled with cerebrospinal fluid are located in the center of the brain mass. The fluid which is produced in the ventricles cushions the brain, distributes nutrients, and collects waste.

Thalamus. The thalamus is located alongside the ventricles in the center of the brain mass between the two hemispheres. It is responsible for pain management and sensory detection.

Hypothalamus. The hypothalamus regulates the metabolism, manages the autonomic functions of the nervous system, and controls the activity of the pituitary, indirectly controlling body temperature, thirst, and hunger.

The brain's functions that have thus far been mapped by western medicine have been strictly based on physical representations of cause and effect. This means that, when they were mapping the brain, they would test an area to see the effect and would consequently map that function to that area. Each person has to be mapped individually using an MRI conducted with appropriate stimulation, if for example surgery is contemplated, because the exact location of the control for any particular function varies. The approximate area is what is known.

The cells of the brain

At the cellular level, there are two types of cells in the brain and spinal column, glial cells and neurons. The spinal column, although not considered part of the brain proper, is an extension of the brain in many ways. It is there to help transfer information back and forth between the body and the brain.

Neurons in the brain are made up of three distinct sections. At the head are the dendrites that connect to other cells. The dendrites are like tentacles that branch out from a cell body that contains one nucleus. An axon that can vary in length extends from the same cell body. There are axon terminals at the end of the axon. Axons carry nerve signals to and from the cell body.

The glial cells are very different from the neurons. They have no active part in cognition. Glia provide structure, insulation, support, and perform other functions for the neurons. Glial cells amount to about 90 percent of the cells in the brain.

Everything you have just read describes the physical components of the brain. The mind, however, is an altogether different business. As much as we tend to use the terms interchangeably, the mind and the brain are not the same thing. The brain is a tangible organ that you can touch and feel. The mind, however, is intangible, and is more of a mental construct than a physical object.

The mind uses memory and extrapolation (which can be referred to as imagination) to develop a kind of pseudo-reality inside our head. The mind uses algorithms based on occurrences in the real world and which are then extrapolated from to understand and predict future outcomes.

What we retain in our brain and the way we retain it are not exactly the way we usually think it is. All of it, including what we smell and hear, is subject to interpretation before it is stored as memory. This is true no matter how vehemently you believe that you remember things exactly the way they occurred. For instance, what we have seen with our eyes is not what we remember; rather, what we remember is an impression of what we have seen. That's how it is for most people.

The rare few who remember things exactly as they see it are described as having photographic memories. However, photographic memory can be learned and practiced. The issue isn't really about having a photographic memory, which is on one end of the spectrum, or having a processed memory, which is on the other end. The trick is to have a healthy balance of both. This doesn't mean choosing to remember some things in one way and other things in another way. Instead, it is that you remember all things in both raw or processed forms but to different degrees in two different phases of your brain.

Six hacks for the physical brain

To hack your mind, you also have to make sure that your brain is working at its best. Hacking the physical brain is fairly easy, but we rarely take the actions necessary.

If you use a little discipline to do these six things, you can supercharge the physical functioning of your brain. Do these, and you will find your brain (and mind) working better:

1. Balance your eating habits and diet.
2. Supply your brain with plenty of oxygen.
3. Drink plenty of water.
4. Sleep well.
5. Wake up before 5 a.m.
6. Get a healthy dose of sunlight every day, even in winter.

So, let's look at these more closely.

Your brain is only as good as what you eat

"You are what you eat." Everything you ingest is converted into energy, nutrients, or waste products. What is absorbed is used up or stored, and what is toxic is discarded or it accumulates. Just because something is bad for you doesn't mean all of it is excreted. Some of it remains.

You can look at it this way – if you ingested arsenic, which is highly toxic, it won't be flushed out. Instead, it is absorbed into your tissues, damaging the body at a cellular level and eventually causing death. Just because your body doesn't use something doesn't mean it is expelled from the system.

The bottom line is that everything you eat affects not only your body but also your brain. Often your brain is even more sensitive to what you ingest than the rest of your physical body.

If you eat in a healthy way, all will be well. If you eat junk, your systems deteriorate. Since this is not a book on diets, I won't go into the effects of junk food except to say that the brain deteriorates when it is fed "junk." When the physical brain deteriorates, the mind is diminished.

Most notable, however, the mind works best when it is not fueled by 100 percent glucose or glycogen. The best source of energy for the brain is a mix of ketones and glucose in a ratio between 70:30 and 80:20. Ketones are the by-product of fat metabolism. You can't take a supplement for this, but you can change the foods you eat, and how often you eat them, to trigger your body's own systems to generate ketones at moderate levels.

Ketones can replace glucose as a temporary source of fuel for the brain. Over the course of human history, we have begun consuming increasing amounts of carbohydrates which readily convert to glucose and then to fat for storage. When we give the brain a constant supply of glucose, the brain doesn't make a fuss, and just takes what it is given. It functions fairly well on glucose – but remember we aren't here to merely function, we are here to hack the mind, and to do that we should make sure that the brain is functioning at optimal levels. And the brain functions at its best when burning ketones as fuel.

If you want to learn more about ketones, Google it, or talk to someone who has adopted a ketogenic lifestyle. Otherwise, simply pay attention to how you feel when you eat carbohydrates, sugars, proteins, fats, and pay attention to how well your brain functions.

The brain needs a constant source of energy. For an organ that weighs just 2 percent of the weight of an average person (who weighs 150 pounds), it consumes more than 20 percent of the total energy the body consumes. It is the most energy-intensive organ in the body.

Also, the brain needs an energy source that is stable. In children who have poor energy profiles, experiencing repeated spikes and dips in blood sugar levels throughout the day, the brain starts to suffer, and scientists have begun to find evidence of the damage.

Researchers have found conclusive evidence that carbohydrates and high sugar diets diminish the brain's health and consequently reduce the mind's power and potential. Insulin spikes from sudden and temporary sugar highs are bad for the brain. The only way to give the brain a stable source of energy is to stop consuming carbohydrates and sugars, which are converted into glucose and glycogen, and, instead, to supply the brain with ketones which are the byproduct of metabolizing fats. Ketones are the brain's super food.

Ask any marathon runner and they will tell you that the carbohydrates they load up on are burned off less than a quarter of the way into a marathon. All the carbohydrates that are converted directly into glycogen and stored in the muscles and liver for easy access only amount to about 1,400 calories. Once that has been used up, the body's real power metabolism kicks in. All the fat that has been stored in adipose tissue all over the body begins to be metabolized. When this kicks in, runners will tell you that they feel energized, their brain gets clear, and the competitive spirit kicks in.

The brain on fat is a powerful computer. All the technology that scientists try to come up with can't even come close to what the brain can do the moment it is running in top form. The first step is to give it a stable, consistent, and powerful source of energy. When the human body eats what it naturally evolved to consume, instead of junk and processed foods, the ideal 70:30 or 80:20 ketone-to-glucose ratio is easily achieved, because of the lower amounts of glucose and carbohydrates in those foods.

If you can't follow a diet that triggers the production of ketones from fats, then, at the very least, avoid foods with a high glycemic index (GI). The glycemic index rates how quickly a food will raise the glucose level of the blood. When the blood is given a shot of glucose from eating a high GI food, insulin is released to mop it all up, causing a spike in insulin levels. Insulin is the key to moving glucose into cells where it can be converted into energy. Without insulin, glucose can't enter the cells to be converted to energy. When the body detects too much sugar in the blood, insulin is released to convert it. Two things then happen: cells take on more glucose, and insulin stops the metabolism of fat. By eating lower GI foods or foods with carbohydrates that enter the bloodstream more slowly, you can avoid that insulin spike – and avoid putting the brakes on the fat metabolism which produces those ketones that the brain functions so well on.

Get more oxygen to your brain

All of us breathe from the moment we come into this world to the moment we check out, yet nearly all of us get that simple process wrong, and pay the price for it in poor health, low energy, and less than optimal brain functioning.

Just as the brain uses 20 percent of the body's energy, the brain also uses 20 percent of the total oxygen consumed by the body. It is, by far, the largest user of oxygen among all the organs, systems, and processes of the body.

You need to ask yourself what happens when you don't get enough oxygen. The answer is that your brain gets foggy, among all the other effects that are not good for you. The typical person, especially someone who doesn't work out at least once every other day, is likely to be breathing incorrectly, resulting in insufficient oxygen intake, which means his or her brain is perpetually running on empty.

The moment you start to focus on breathing better, you will instantly see an improvement in your cognitive functioning. There are two basic ways to deliver more oxygen to the brain: breathe better, and increase circulation and absorption.

Breathe better

The first thing to do is to relearn how to breathe properly. Breathing is typically handled by the subconscious part of the brain, specifically, a part of the brain situated at the intersection of the brain and the brainstem, the medulla oblongata. This part of the brain subconsciously handles the respiration rate and even tidal breathing (breathing that occurs in a resting state).

Our body gets used to and acclimates to different conditions, even shallow breathing. The body's homeostatic mechanisms are designed to help the body acclimate to the resources available to it. If, for instance, one is placed in an oxygen-poor environment, the body would start to acclimate by shutting down various systems, and it would start to conserve resources in a way that would allow the body and brain to survive in those conditions. However, just because you can function or are surviving does not mean that you are at peak functioning.

If you are overweight, the capacity of your lungs may be restricted so that you aren't able to expand your lungs to their optimal size to take in enough oxygen to function well. Your systems will gradually begin to make do with reduced oxygen, and you acclimate to a partial hypoxic state. That reduced state includes the diminished state of your brain. If your brain is starved of oxygen, brain-related problems arise. This can present itself as foggy behavior, inaccurate analysis of issues, or even as a depressed state.

For most people, one way to gain an immediate mental edge is to start making a concerted effort to breathe better. Here are three things you can do to help yourself improve the physical act of breathing:

1. Improve your posture.

Realigning your spinal column, by sleeping on a firm surface, will help align the muscles that hold your spine in place. Then, when you are up and about, your thoracic cavity will have the optimal space available for your lungs to expand freely.

2. Reduce the size of your belly.

When your belly doesn't weigh down on your diaphragm as you sit, impinging on your diaphragm, you will improve the volume of your lung capacity.

3. Walk more.

Walking at a brisk pace deepens your breathing and strengthens your diaphragm and intercostal musculature. This allows greater breathing volume, even at rest. The increased muscle tone also allows you to deepen your breathing, increasing the volume of air that is taken in, while reducing the effort required.

The brain operates more effectively when it is receiving higher volumes of oxygen, at a more stable rate, without interruptions. However, do not force your breathing as that alters the concentration of carbon dioxide in your system and changes your oxygen intake levels.

Circulation and absorption

When we're talking about ways to improve oxygen uptake to the brain, we can't just talk about increasing the amount of oxygen we breathe in, we also need to improve the efficiency of moving that extra oxygen around the body and absorbing it into the cells where it is needed to increase cellular activity. In other words, to increase the amount of oxygen that reaches the brain, we need to improve blood circulation and the absorption of oxygen.

Circulation keeps nutrients, oxygen, and water constantly on the move so that all tissues in your body are able to get what they need to function efficiently. When one has poor circulation, oxygen doesn't get to the parts it needs to and carbon dioxide isn't removed. Waste from cellular activity remains, poisoning the surrounding tissue. Poor circulation is also a reason for the inefficient movement of particles in the blood that can eventually clog up the arteries and cause build up, eventually constricting the arteries and reducing flow of blood to the area.

In addition to circulation, the proper rate of absorption is another factor in the exchange of nutrients, oxygen, and energy in the body. Energy moves around the body in two forms, as fatty acids or glucose. Oxygen is carried by the hemoglobin in red blood cells, and nutrients are dissolved and carried in the blood.

Absorption refers to how the cells receive the energy and nutrients that have been delivered to them. Take glucose for instance. Cells do not readily absorb glucose. When the body consumes sugar, it enters the bloodstream, resulting in high levels of sugar in the blood. The sugar remains in the blood until the adrenal gland secretes insulin. That insulin attaches itself to the sugar and unlocks the cell allowing the sugar to enter. At that point, the sugar gets absorbed by the cell. Without absorption, all the food and oxygen in the world is not going to get to the cell where it is needed. That is why you need to optimize what you eat, optimize your circulation so that it all gets to where it's needed, and optimize your absorption so that once it gets there, it gets absorbed.

There are three things you can do to optimize your circulation and the absorption of the oxygen you need for peak brain functioning:

1. Drink plenty of water.
2. Increase blood volume.
3. Work out more.

1. Drink plenty of water

To keep the brain healthy and functioning at peak cognitive and mental condition, you need to keep it well hydrated. Water is essential at every step for the efficient movement and absorption of oxygen and all the other nutrients the brain relies on.

Water is the single most important component of the body, and even more so of the brain. The body is made up of 60 percent water on average, while the brain is about 73 percent water, and muscles are about 80 percent water. And that is just the water required to maintain the physical form. More water is needed to nourish, clean, lubricate, and cool the brain. All this adds up to a lot of water – both still and cycling through the body's systems. Don't think of water as something you consume to retain. Think of water as something that flows through you.

If you are drinking enough water but don't have the proper salinity levels in your system, that water is going to come right out of you without ever hydrating you at the cellular level. Without salts and electrolytes, water cannot be effectively absorbed into the cells.

The brain operates at an optimal salinity, outside of which its electrical activity diminishes drastically. Without that electrical activity there is no living brain. In fact, it is the defining quality of a living brain. A brain without electrical activity is "brain dead." It's not a stretch to say that water, salt, and electrolytes are required for a fully functioning brain and a truly "hacked" mind.

If you are concerned that you are drinking too much water, you can add hydration salts or a slice of lemon to the water you drink. That will replace electrolytes lost through perspiration or too much water intake. Mineral water is best. Avoid RO (Reverse Osmosis) water which will leech nutrients from your system and leave you worse off than before you drank it. It will also rapidly dilute the salinity across your systems.

Water is the key to optimal brain function. The healthier your brain, the more powerful your mind becomes. If you doubt the importance of water, stop drinking water for just one day and see how foggy and delirious you feel. (No, do NOT do that – I was only trying to make the point of just how critical water is to your well-being.)

Water does several things that boost the performance of your brain. Water improves cellular function and efficiency. Water acts as the "filler" in your cells to maintain their shape and keep them plumped up. It reduces the viscosity of your blood, allowing your blood to flow better. Blood plasma, which is more than half of total blood volume, is 90 percent water. Water reduces stress on the heart. If your blood is too thick, it clogs up, putting a strain on your heart, while it reduces the flow of nutrients, oxygen, and energy to everywhere, including your brain.

Water allows the efficient shuttling of toxic by-products out of the system, including out of the brain. Water also improves hepatic function. It allows the movement of toxic waste products out of the cells, tissues, and organs to the renal system. The more water you have, the more you can flush toxins out of the body, keep the brain hydrated, and keep all systems working and functioning efficiently.

2. Increase blood volume

The second thing you need to do to increase circulation and absorption of oxygen is to increase the volume of blood, specifically the volume of red blood cells. More red blood cells means a greater capacity to carry oxygen, and that increased oxygen allows for better metabolism and better brain function. The red of those blood cells is caused by haemoglobin which is an oxygen-carrying protein that contains iron.

There are a few ways to increase red blood cells in the body. A common prescription is to increase heme iron (iron from animal proteins) through dietary considerations. Iron levels can also be increased by taking supplements. Another way to increase the blood's red blood cells is to work out more.

3. Work out more

Working out more is an effective way to increase the levels of oxygen-carrying red blood cells. Physical activity that gets the heart pumping, like running or brisk walking, places a demand on the body, and to satisfy that demand, the body will adapt. One of the ways the body can adapt is to increase the production of hemoglobin to increase the blood's oxygen-carrying capacity.

Some athletes train at higher elevations where there are lower oxygen levels, so that the body is forced to adapt by increasing the production of red blood cells and dilating the capillaries and arteries. In time, those athletes adapt to the lower oxygen environment, and when they return to regular altitudes, they are able to perform better, because they can circulate more oxygen to the muscles.

But you don't need to be an athlete or climb a mountain to increase the amount of oxygen your blood can carry to your brain. The more you move physically, the more circulation you foster, so the third thing you can do to improve circulation and absorption is simply to work out more.

One way to increase something is to create the need for it. Our bodies are built to stabilize according to where we are and what we do. Athletes who train five to eight hours a day build up better muscles and better circulation to adapt to that condition of higher physical activity. That improves the circulation of oxygen- and nutrient-carrying blood, and the absorption of oxygen and nutrients, while increasing stamina, and even speeding up cognitive processes.

Sleep better

To have a fully functioning brain, you need to sleep well – and this does not necessarily mean sleeping more. In some cases, it may actually mean sleeping less. Too much sleep can cloud the brain as it reduces oxygen uptake and keeps the mind sedated for too long.

One of the most important mind hacks is the creation of an environment where your brain can form memories and extract them expeditiously. And that means sleeping well.

A lot of what we consider as having a good brain boils down to how we encode our memories. When you study something, it is of no use to you if you can't remember it or associate it with something in the past or the future. Remembering all the experiences that you go through in life is the best way to create a powerful database of knowledge, which, if encoded properly, can trigger the relevant associative memories.

When you get an idea or random memory, what is happening in the background is that one memory has been associated with another, and when you trigger one, the other is triggered as well. For people who can't control their minds that can translate into a mind in chaos.

Have you ever played the word game where your opponent says one word and you say the first thing that pops into your head? Then they say the first thing that pops into theirs, and on it goes. That is the same way your synapses fire to give you seemingly random thoughts.

Each memory is stored in a web of connections. The more connections there are to that memory, the easier it becomes to access that memory. Those connections are made while you sleep. When you make a memory while you are awake, that memory is encoded chemically by connections designed to be short-term.

To go from short-term memory to long-term memory, the chemical encoding of the memory needs to be replicated in neuronal connections. These are electro-chemical connections attached to memories that are already stored long-term in the brain. If the memory is completely new and has no relationship to what you already know, it gets harder to remember. The way we get around that is to use analogies and similes to give us a shadow of similarity which allows us to create neurons that connect to existing neurons. That's why it is always easier to understand things that are built on things we already know.

It makes sense that the more neurons there are, the better. The average brain contains a billion neurons in a lifetime. When these neurons are used, they are fortified, and more connections are made. When these neurons are not used, eventually, they are broken up and discarded. For example, if you use an access code constantly, you will remember it readily, but if you don't use it for some time, chances are that you will forget it.

The key, then, is to make as many neurons as possible, and the brain makes these neurons when we are asleep. One of the side effects of these neurons being made while we sleep is that we have dreams of randomly combined sequences. That is happening while different neurons are activated as they are being connected to the memory that is being formed.

The more neurons are connected together, the stronger the memory. And that is advanced by having more sleep. The longer you sleep, the more it promotes neurogenesis, the creation of neurons, loaded up with the memories of the day.

Sleep also helps keep the mind rested, and gives the circulation time to remove toxins that accumulate during the process of energy synthesis in the brain. Cells in the brain metabolize their own energy and this energy metabolism creates byproducts that need to be gotten rid of. Although waste products are removed gradually during the day, when you sleep, they are removed much more efficiently. That is one of the reasons you wake up "fresh" in the morning.

The quantity of time you sleep is not the only important factor in supercharging your brain and hacking your mind to do better. The time of night you sleep and the time you wake up are also important. Some of the most successful people I know have one thing in common – they all wake up before 5 a.m. or before the sun rises.

You have to find your own ideal wake up time and your ideal going to bed time. There are different guidelines that can help you figure that out. I would suggest that there are two magic numbers when it comes to sleep – four and eight. You should get either four hours of sleep or eight. I typically sleep for four hours every night between midnight and 4 a.m. When I catch the right cycle, I wake up energized and usually before the alarm goes off. Once you make it a habit, you will automatically wake up and feel energized and refreshed. Of course, the best single way to control your wake-up time is to control when you go to bed.

Get some sunshine every day

Last, but not least, expose yourself to more sunlight. We tend to underestimate the importance of sunshine in our life. Exposure to sun is responsible for supplying the body with vitamin D. Sunlight regulates the production of melatonin in the brain, which in turn regulates sleep cycles. Sunlight also causes the release of endorphins, the brain's own mood enhancing chemicals, necessary for a positive and energetic response to life. Sunlight has numerous other chemical effects on the body and brain.

The best sunlight for this is when the sun is just over the horizon, about 30 minutes after sunrise. Midday sun is fine, but it also has the highest levels of UV rays which is not good for your skin and can damage your eyes unless you are wearing eye protection. If you do go out at midday, make sure you have ample protection from harmful UV rays.

Morning sunlight, on the other hand, is something that naturally energizes and invigorates your mind. Human beings evolved to wake naturally to the bluer tones of early morning light. Many ancient traditions include morning rituals that recognize and pay tribute to the life-giving power of the earliest morning hours.

So, wake early and rise up to greet the day with a mind and brain ready to be at its best.

Afterword

The human mind is a framework based on a physical organ. It is more powerful than any contraption that the human hand can build or imagine, because the mind is the culmination of billions of minds evolving over billions of years, gradually getting better with each iteration. No CPU or computer can do better.

The reason we need to hack our mind is not that it is inadequate or faulty but because we need to find the best way to control it so it can do what it has the potential to do. That great potential is hidden under layers of distraction. From TV to constant consumerism to social media, we spend a lot of our time being persuaded to believe we are that which we are not.

Einstein, Newton, Hawking, Jobs, and countless others have had the same three-pound human brain that you and I have. Yet they made a difference only because they did the same thing you are instinctively trying to do – master the mind. "Hacking it" is really just the present era's colloquial way of expressing the same desire and intention that humankind has always had, that of bringing the mind in line with and under the direction of the *"I."*

* * *

I hope this book has brought *you* closer to *your mind*... and closer to fulfilling your dreams. Best of luck.

Memory Improvement
The Secrets of Memory Manipulation Revealed

Memory Improvement
The Secrets of Memory Manipulation Revealed

Retrain Your Brain to Improve Your Memory and Discover Your Unlimited Memory Potential

Memory and Learning Exercises to Remember More

Kyle Faber

Memory Improvement – The Secrets of Memory Manipulation Revealed

Retrain Your Brain to Improve Your Memory and Discover Your Unlimited Memory Potential

Copyright © 2018 Kyle Faber

All rights reserved. No portion of this book may be reproduced, stored in a retrieval system, or transmitted in any form or by any means – electronic, mechanical, photocopy, recording, scanning, or other – except for brief quotations in critical reviews or articles, without prior written permission of the publisher.

Published by CAC Publishing LLC.

ISBN 978-1-950010-17-2 paperback

ISBN 978-1-950010-16-5 eBook

Introduction: An Evolving Memory

Improving your memory isn't just about remembering phone numbers or where you put your keys. By remembering to look after your memory, you can boost the performance of your mind so that more information will be available more quickly, you can make better decisions, and achieve your goals more effectively.

In recent decades, there has been an explosion in our understanding of how the brain works, how memory is encoded and stored, and how much mental capacity we really have. This increase in knowledge has come from two directions. On one side, there are the hard sciences of neuroscience, biology, and genetics. On the other side are the softer sciences of psychology and philosophy. This book balances both.

Memory is not a single thing. We have a variety of types of memory, which can be broadly categorized as *sensory memories*, *short-term memories,* or *long-term memories*. Sensory memory is the shortest lasting memory of all, lasting just fractions of a second, long enough for a sense to process its input. Short-term memory has a very different purpose than long-term memory and is encoded differently in the mind.

Short-term memory is encoded rapidly and is meant to last a short time, less than 30 seconds. Long-term memory takes longer to stitch together but is meant to last indefinitely. If content went directly into long term memory, that memory item would not be available for a few minutes immediately after it occurred as it is being encoded into the long-term memory. Also, there would be no process to filter the important from the unimportant, so we would be overwhelmed with a massive amount of unnecessary memories. Both would result in a very incoherent mental experience.

The first type of long-term memory is *explicit memory* (or *declarative memory*) – which is what we tend to think of when we talk about "memory." It requires conscious thought. It's what we try to specifically store in memory. It's what we are using when someone tells us their date of birth or phone number and we put in the effort to remember the information. Generally, this is the kind of memory people are talking about when they say they want to improve their memory, but there are many other types of memory that are equally important to keep functioning at optimal levels.

A second type of long-term memory is *implicit memory* (or *non-declarative memory*). These are the things we remember automatically, without conscious thought, almost as second nature once learned. *Procedural memory*, remembering how to do a complex activity without conscious attention, is a very common type of implicit memory. Once someone has learned to read, drive a car, or tie shoelaces, through repetition, it becomes procedural memory. *Muscle memory*, or *motor learning*, is a type of procedural memory, and is a huge part of the practical side of memory. Everything from walking on a regular pavement to balancing on a gymnasts' beam, and riding a bike are examples of muscle memory.

There are also memories that have to do with who you are – your *episodic memory* – all your experiences, your name, what you look like, who you are, where you live, who the significant members of your family are, and so on. These are the memories that make up our personal and collective histories.

There are the memories of what we want which keep us moving toward goals, and the memories of what we don't want which remind us to move away from the undesired.

And then there are the memories of hard data, facts, and information that aren't drawn from personal experience, our *semantic memory*. This is most of what we learned in the classroom. This is most of what we know for our professions or our interests. This is our general knowledge of the world and our culture.

Memory is not only the foundation of all of your knowledge, but it is also the center of your social life, it is the core of your profession, and it is the soul of your desire. Without memory, you would not know who that man or woman is that you see in the mirror each morning. You need memory to associate that face in the mirror with a set of values, beliefs, experiences, and relationships with others. You need a great memory to do all that and more.

The evolution of the brain

The brain's evolutionary path has not been one of random mutation and adaptation; it has been one of gradual development driven by internal desires, and by needs triggered by the external environment, and by the challenges presented by our surroundings that we need to overcome to achieve our objectives. The brain's evolution has been largely responsible for humans rising from being third rate scavengers (after the lions and hyenas) in the wild to claiming the pinnacle of the food chain as the dominant species.

Early hominids, who were our ancestors about two million years ago, used to trail lions and hyenas, not to hunt them, but to wait in the shadows to scavenge what was left after they were done with their prey. Bones were all that were usually left, from which they picked the scrapings, but they also began to use those bones as tools.

Those tools helped them expand their capabilities – and that brought them better food. Better food and nutrition allowed the brains of early humans to develop. The more their brains developed, the more powerful the tools they developed, accelerating their rise to the top.

The skull of the man-ape, *Australopithecus*, from two to three million years ago, has a cranial vault that was comparatively tiny – a mere 490 cubic centimeters. A million (or two) years later, *Homo Erectus*, or the Java Man, had a slightly larger cranial vault of about 935 cubic centimeters. Then, just 100,000 years ago, *Homo Sapiens Neanderthalensis*, Neanderthal Man, had a larger cranial vault that measured approximately 1,600 cubic centimeters, even larger than present-day humans. Present day man has a slightly smaller cranial capacity of 1,350 cubic centimeters. The decreased size is the result of the increased efficiency of the modern human brain.

The evolution of memory

Different features and types of memory developed over millions of years, in response to needs that emerged as species evolved. *Spatial memory* came about because early species that had developed ambulatory skills needed to know where they were and where they were going. Spatial memory prevents you from going around in circles, not knowing where you are at any given point in time. It is also crucial to the ability to forage for food and for venturing out into the world to hunt and explore. Spatial memory developed because there was a need for it.

As the brain developed further, other skills and abilities were added to it. *Feature memory* allows us to remember what tree bears what fruit by recognizing the features of the tree. It allows us to remember a location by remembering the features of the surroundings. Feature memory allows us to distinguish one kind of plant from another so that we can realize that, under the ground, a specific plant will have a tasty root vegetable. Memory evolved as was needed for the tasks that were asked of it until we now have the various powerful faculties that we, as a species, take for granted.

Even for an individual, the basis for any mental improvement or memory enhancement is actively pursuing a need or desire that requires it. If you want to memorize phone numbers, but you continue to use your smartphone's contact function to "remember" phone numbers, then you are not really acting on your desires. There isn't really any need to develop the ability to remember those numbers.

As various types of memory developed in response to the needs of early man, two related things were happening in the background. As the brain developed more capabilities, it needed more capacity. As mentioned, the cranial capacity of the early biped humanoids grew bigger, indicating the larger volume of its contents, the brain.

As more memory and processing capabilities became available, a better system for organizing and prioritizing the vast amounts of new data was needed. The brain developed a system of preferential encoding of memory or biased competition. The memories that are encoded for long-term storage and are the most easily accessible are those with the highest need of being retained. There is a sort of competition between individual memories as to which gets encoded. The memory with the strongest bias or emotion is the one that gets more connections during the encoding process and thus has a better chance of being remembered.

In other words, we remember what has aroused and motivated us. Hunger arouses us to remember where to find food, and fear motivates us to remember where to find shelter and to remember what dangers to avoid. Those are powerful basic instincts, and they exert significant control over what we remember and what we forget.

With a system in place to determine what was important to remember, the brain's development leapt forward. That system became the basis of what the brain remembers – and that determined how the species evolved. Imagine if we remembered how to find our cave, but not how to find our prey. Or if we remembered every detail of the shapes of a cloud, but not the face of someone who threatened our safety. What would happen? How the brain knows what to remember has been an important factor in the success of our evolving development.

Our brain selects out as important to remember those memories which are tied to powerful emotions. We tend to remember mistakes more than achievements, and bad events more than good, because that helps to keep us from repeating those. We remember conflict and uncomfortable events because fear is a powerful emotion that marks out situations that are better avoided. It is valuable for us to remember bad experiences and dangerous events, but it can also become debilitating if when we go overboard with that.

If you are like many people and believe you have a bad memory, think again. You don't. You can prove it to yourself just by remembering something bad that happened to you. That proves that your memory circuits are working just fine. You simply need to realize that you are motivated to remember some things but not others.

Understanding that the brain evolved to remember things based on how much they affect you gives you your first tool for expanding your capacity to remember. If you want to increase how much you remember, then you need to be in a state that finds the information you want to remember useful, important, even urgent. So, the first tool to improve your memory is to understand your emotional and mental state, and your motivation for remembering something. You can't expect to remember anything that you are approaching in a half-hearted way. Are you motivated enough to remember it?

Ironically, it is memory, itself, that helps you remember what you are motivated to move toward, whether that's a better memory or some other thing. The ability to remember objectives, *goal memory*, allows you to project what will happen next and move toward it. It allows you to learn from experience, so you can circumvent poor outcomes by having goals that keep you on a track toward outcomes that will make you better off. Goal memory is a powerful tool that the human mind uses to imagine a future and then work toward it. It gives you the ability to think about what to have for lunch before you are hungry. It allows you to plan for summer vacation next year while it is still snowing outside.

It isn't an exaggeration to say that when you take charge of your own memories, improving not only how much you remember but also the quality of the memories you choose to make, you are deciding who you will become moving forward. When a pattern of memories forms, that can determine your frame of mind. Putting all your memories together, you have the basis for your mindset and a personality – and that determines your behavior and the path your future will take.

It really doesn't matter if you don't take the time to remember phone numbers, you can get your phone to do that for you. But you can increase the power of your mind by improving your memory. It is not an exaggeration to say that memory is the key to what becomes of you in your own personal evolution, and that it is one of the keys to your destiny.

Chapter 1: The Brain, Neurons, and Memory

A basic understanding of the physical brain and the lifecycle of neurons provides clues on how to have a robust and effective memory. Over a hundred billion neurons and significantly more glial cells make up the three-pound mass of the brain.

Neurons, which are the primary signaling cells of the human body and brain, range from just a few microns in length inside the folds of the brain to a few feet in length along the spinal column and spreading across the network. These neurons connect to each other – by association, the single most important organizing and operational feature of the brain and memory. Each neuron connects with anywhere from a thousand to tens of thousands of neighboring neurons. *Interneurons*, one of the main types of neurons, form connections between neurons. Interneurons are also known as *association neurons*.

Each neuron that comes into being is useless until it is in place and connected to other neurons. An individual neuron, with its bit of information, only becomes useful when it connects with another neuron that has another bit of information. Each neuron is connected to another neuron across a void called a *synapse* – transmitters need to jump this gap to complete the connection.

A neuron can connect to thousands of other neurons, but that connection is not physical – it is air-gapped – which is a pretty ingenious part of the structure. If the connection were continuous, there would be information flowing everywhere indiscriminately. A continuous connection between neurons would result in an incoherent and useless jumble of noise.

Instead, electrical and chemical signals have to jump across the synaptic gap. A certain threshold of effort must be applied before information is transmitted across that gap. As an electrical impulse moves from the *soma* through the *axon* to the *terminus*, it signals *vesicles* to release *neurotransmitters*. These neurotransmitters leave the *axon terminus* and jump the synaptic gap to the connected neuron.

When neurons "fire," they fire in unison and in sequence. That's why we think of an idea as a moment of illumination – there is literally a light that flashes – and you can see it on an MRI.

On the other hand, a neuron in isolation has the sole purpose of holding a fragment of information – which, by itself, is essentially useless. It's like taking the *Declaration of Independence* and keeping just one letter of the whole document, let's say the "D" from "Declaration." That D, on its own, has no context, could mean anything, and therefore has no real meaning.

In the same way, individual bits of information floating around in your head without context and association are useless, and only take up resources without adding any value. When the bits of information are brought together, context and association give meaning to the information (i.e. memory), narrowing down its purpose and place in the brain. That means that when you want to remember something, try to put it into a context – give each fragment of information "meaning" by anchoring it to something that you already know.

Of course, not all neurons are designed to store fragments of memory. Neurons, in general, are cells that send, receive, and relay electrochemical messages, but there are different types of neurons with different roles. Most neurons in the brain are tasked with performing motor functions, while others perform sensory functions. *Sensory neurons* relay sensory information, and *motor neurons* send signals down the spine to individual muscles and muscle groups to generate action in those muscles. Sensory neurons account for less than one percent of the total neurons available, while motor neurons account for close to ten percent of brain mass.

Overwhelmingly, the rest of the cells of the nervous system and brain are actually non-electrochemical brain cells called *glial cells* that do a lot of support work unrelated to the storage or action potential of neurons. Up to 90 percent of the brain are glial cells. *Glial cells*, or *glia*, do things like digest dead neurons, supply nutrients and oxygen to neurons, manufacture protective sheeting, and help to provide an environment for the flaccid neurons preventing them from tangling with each other. The overall physical health of the brain and memory is tied up with the health and functioning of those glial cells.

Until recently, it was believed that we were born with all the neurons we would ever have in our lifetime, and that when a neuron died it was never replaced. However, it now only beginning to be understood that neurons have a much more complex life cycle than formerly believed. We aren't born with a specific set of neurons that never changes throughout our life, except to die. Rather, some are born, some live, and some die. *Neurogenesis* and *neuroapoptosis* are about the birth and death of neurons. *Neuroplasticity* is about the way neurons change over a lifetime.

The birth of neurons: *neurogenesis*

Neurogenesis refers to the birth of neurons, the foundational circuitry of the brain. The first thing to remember is that you are not born with a full and fixed set of neurons, and you don't spend your life with a predetermined number. It is now understood that new neurons continue to be created throughout life, and that you are not born with all the neurons you would ever have, as was previously believed. Although human babies are born with an enormous number of neurons, and many of those will stay functional until the person dies, there are also new neurons created every day. It has been observed in recent research that there is a special type of stem cell responsible for the birth of new neurons.

For our purposes, though, what is most important to understand is that the birth of new neurons is triggered by what we do, learn, think, and experience. In neurogenesis, cells in the brain respond to the stimuli of learning a new skill or repeating it frequently. When something new is learned, new cells are formed in one part of the brain and then moved to the area of the brain where they are needed. The hippocampus, the area of the brain responsible for consolidating and transferring memory into long-term storage, is also where neurogenesis is found to occur. This generation of new neuronal cells is a lifelong process.

If you want a brain and memory that functions at its best, then you need to make sure to stimulate the birth of new neurons by learning and doing new things. Learn a new language. Do puzzles.

Try something completely new. Your memory will be better for it.

The importance of the brain's capacity to generate new neurons is nowhere more evident than when there has been an injury to the brain. From the perspective of adaptation after injury, neurogenesis is a subset of neuroplasticity. As long as the brain is supplied with the right nutrients, adequate levels of oxygen saturation, and a sufficient supply of blood, neurogenesis can occur even in old age.

For instance, if a stroke victim has damage in the area of the brain that controls walking, repeated practice in re-learning to walk triggers neurogenesis. Those new neurons are moved to the location in the brain involved with the ability to walk, that is, to the location in the brain that "remembers" how to walk.

For an older person, that process of re-learning after a stroke can take significantly longer if there is suboptimal cardiac and pulmonary health, and reduced muscle mass which makes it harder to complete physiotherapy. If all these are overcome, the person can regain the ability to walk, but returning to full pre-stroke gait and strength takes practice and repetition.

Neurogenesis is important for everyone, not just when there is injury or damage. It is central to having a good, optimally functioning memory. Maintaining a good memory is about creating new neurons and new connections, whether that's for new memories or simply keeping old memories alive. If, for any reason, you became unable to trigger neurogenesis, you would not be able to create any new long-term memories from that point forward. And anything new that you learn (or re-learn) would not be available to you.

Once it has been created, the new neuron needs to be moved into its final place. This occurs in a couple of different ways that are still being studied. One way is through the use of chemical signaling. New neurons are guided by adhesion molecules along existing migratory pathways until they get to where they are going. Much of this happens as you asleep, and, as new neurons creep against existing neurons, some may be triggered, causing dreams of the content it has triggered. New neurons may also crawl along radial glia as they migrate to their new sites.

Memory by association is so effective because new neurons don't just materialize to fill in an empty spot – they need to be located near or attached to other neurons. To be attached to another neuron, the information needs to be related. This is why most of the strategies in this book are based on associating a new memory with an old one.

Any given memory has just a one in three chance of getting to its optimal storage location, of being stored in the best place for it to be recalled easily later. This is one of the reasons we have little gaps in our memories, the reason we forget things we feel we should remember easily, and the reason behind much of the confusion we experience.

The implications for improving your memory are clear. You should perfect each memory so that it is not only well formed but it is also more likely to arrive at the best location for it to be stored in. Strategies to accomplish this include everything from paying attention to staying in good health.

The death of neurons: *neuroapoptosis*

Neuroapoptosis is the exact opposite of neurogenesis – it is the death of neurons in the brain, spinal column, or elsewhere in the central nervous system. Cells in the nervous system have unusually long lives, starting at pre-birth, and surviving until death unless there is a serious injury to the brain.

By contrast, other cells in the human body have a lifespan that is shorter than that of the person, living anywhere from just a few days to a few months. Of course, the full potential lifespan of any cell applies only when the body is healthy and under optimal conditions. If there are other factors like suboptimal nutrition, substance abuse, and injury, cells, including neurons, are not likely to live out their full lifespans.

The benefit of having cells that never die is that memories can last a lifetime. The downside is that the cerebral environment, therefore, has not been designed to automatically replace specific cells when they are damaged or die. The only way to generate new neurons is to do new things, travel to new places, experience new sensations. This includes re-learning old things to replace damaged neurons, for example, in the event of a stroke.

Even though most people think that fading memory has to do with the physical attrition of brain cells, this is not usually true. When you forget something, it's not because your brain cell has died. It's because you are not making use of it, so the number of connections that lead to the memory have been reduced to conserve resources. The cells that hold your memories require a lot of energy, oxygen, and nutrients to maintain themselves over their lifespan, so the brain cannot afford to expend resources on memories that are not important enough to be used. So, this means that while the neuron housing the memory may still be alive, the pathways to retrieve the memory may be disappearing.

The living and changing brain: *neuroplasticity*

Neuroplasticity refers to the brain's ability to physically change throughout life, altering with experiences, learnings, and injuries. The principal way this occurs is through the birth and death of neurons, and the changing connections between neurons.

Every experience you have reverberates throughout the brain and causes changes to it. Your brain is never the same from one day to the next. As Heraclitus said, "A man never steps in the same river twice, the river is never the same, and neither is the man." Heraclitus could as well have said that each new experience that a man encounters changes the makeup and map of his mind.

In the wake of an injury, there are a number of ways that neurons are either replaced or repaired. The replacement method of repair, after the death of a group of neurons, is by re-learning the information that was contained in those neurons. That triggers the birth of new neurons to replace the dead or damaged ones.

The second method utilizes what is most commonly meant by the term "neuroplasticity." In the event of damage, the brain continues to use the old neuron but forms new connections in different locations to the existing neuron. This can only occur if the injury has not fully damaged the neuron and only some of its connections have been affected.

You can think of it in the following way. If you build a city with roads that go from city hall to the mayor's mansion, there will be more than one way to get from one location to the other. If one of the roads were demolished, you could build another one to add to the number of available routes to get from one to the other, in case there were traffic jams or other obstacles. However, if one of the buildings, the mansion or city hall, were destroyed, then an entirely new building would have to be constructed. It wouldn't be enough to pave a new road.

In the same way, if the neuron is not damaged, connections can be made with other neurons to connect to it in faster and more diverse ways. If the neuron, itself, is damaged, an entirely new neuron is needed – and learning (or re-learning) is required for that.

Neuroplasticity helps to keep the brain's thoughts and functions intact when there is damage to neurons. It also allows you to change or override something you have already learned, such as an ingrained habit that you want to change. A good way to change an established habit is to extinguish past connections (through dis-use) and to create new connections through learning and practicing the desired behavior – and that process precisely describes what neuroplasticity is really all about.

The changes described by the term neuroplasticity occur whether you make those changes intentionally or not. As you take in and accumulate new information and experiences, and have different thoughts and feelings, the map of neurons and their connections changes, and that changes your brain.

The process of improving your memory is subject to the degree of fixedness of the neurons and the various structures that make up the functional core of the brain. Some elements are hardwired and are replicated from one generation to the next, while others are there to adapt to current circumstances. You can improve your memory, within those constraints, by working with those areas designed to change.

You can even change how effectively memories form, if you practice and place demands on the brain to increase your ability to remember. "Willing" and "trying" are not enough – you need to do the things that increase your brain's ability to create and transport the new neurons into place, and that create more connections between neurons.

In a real sense, you can make yourself into whoever you choose to be (including someone with well-developed memory and mental processes), because everything that makes up who you are boils down to synaptic connections between neurons, and the memories you create that define who you are.

You can take control of this natural neuroplasticity, and, in turn, the quality of your own memory. You can enhance the process of neurogenesis and increase your memory powers – with the right knowledge and exercises to do it. The more nimble you keep your brain, the easier it is to create synapses between neurons, making more of those connections that are at the very heart of memory by association.

Setting the stage for a better memory

If you just jump in and start messing with the neural connections and the synapses in your brain, you probably won't have much success. As with anything, the first thing you need to do is realize that you have in your own hands the awesome power to make the changes you want. Second, you have to call upon the determination and willpower to take the steps that will accomplish what you want.

Third, you need to believe in the benefits you will gain from changing your brain and improving your memory. The one thing that your subconscious is good at is calculating cost-to-benefit ratios. If you are about to embark on something that appears less worthy compared to what you already have, you will find your subconscious trying to sabotage your efforts internally.

That is one of the reasons people fail at trying to improve or change themselves – they do not believe in what they are doing, and they do not have the facts or a way to prove the benefit to themselves. The currency between your conscious and your subconscious is desire and belief. If you have enough desire and belief, your subconscious will be on board, and will work, behind the scenes, to support your efforts.

There are five specific things you can do to set the stage, to create the best environment, for you to work on having a better memory.

1. Reflect

When you do deep reflection on any subject you are interested in, you are actually triggering activity in the neurons, neuronal pathways, and networks associated with the area you are thinking about. That means that when you reflect on something that you want to change, you are activating that area in your brain. So, when you start to think about what memory does for you, all the reasons you want to improve it, your brain begins to work on that for you, behind the scenes.

2. Identify hindrances

Take some time to identify what blocks you from achieving what you want, a better memory. Is it poor habits, poor nutrition, or constant distraction? Or something else? That will help you to identify where you are at the moment. That will help you plot a path from where you are to where you want to go, and provide you with a direction to take. Sometimes those obstacles are the path – remove them and you find yourself where you want to be.

3. Ask

When you "ask" repeatedly for what you want, your subconscious begins to search through all the things you already know, whether you are aware of it or not, and works on the "problem," looking for a "solution" – for a way to get you what you want. Simply asking for a better memory is a powerful tool, and you should never discount the simple act of asking. You will be surprised by the insights and nudges you may get that'll help you to get that better memory you want.

4. Meditate

Meditating has been proven to put your brain into a malleable and receptive state, a state that promotes neuroplasticity. Meditating will also generally increase the effectiveness of all the things you do to improve your memory.

5. Sleep

A good night's sleep can do wonders for memory. The best sleep comes at the end of a physically active day. This means working out, getting your circulation and breathing pumping. With a vigorous workout, your body releases the right hormones to promote not only deep sleep but also neuron binding.

And remember, before you go to sleep, reflect a little, ask a little, and do a little meditation. That'll set you up with the best conditions for having a better memory.

Chapter 2: The Making of Memories

There are three main processes involved in human memory: encoding, storage (which includes *consolidation*), and retrieval. The retrieval process of memory has its roots in the recording process – you can only remember (retrieve) what has become a lasting memory. That means it is important to understand how memories are formed if you want to have a better memory.

There are three stages in the making of every lasting memory of a real-world event. First, we record sensory input into sensory memory. In a matter of seconds, that is moved into short-term memory. Later, that memory is consolidated and moved into long-term memory. It is possible, if we do it right, to go into the farthest reaches of our mind and find much of what has come across our senses. Normally, though, we only remember what we need to remember.

As many have found, writing things down tends to make it easier to recall something later. The aid to memory doesn't come from writing it down so that it is easier to reference the material later on, but comes about because the act of writing, in itself, tells the brain that the material is "important," and needs to be remembered. The brain will then catalog the memory in a way to make recall easier.

Think about some of the clearest memories you have. Are they good ones – or about things that are disturbing? Why is it that you can only seem to remember the things that have had the greatest impact on you and not the things that are inconsequential?

What we remember is, to a large degree, a function of focus. The brain has the potential to record everything, but only earmarks for remembering what we pay attention to. Because what we pay attention to is determined by the impact it has on us, we remember most readily what has had a significant impact on us.

Just how we remember something is tainted or intensified by the state we were in at the time that the memory was created. It affects how long we will remember it, how easily the memory can be retrieved, and the ways it can be retrieved.

Later, our state of mind as we retrieve the memory is also important. Memories are subject to interpretation as they are recalled and interacted with. Memories are malleable when they have been retrieved. When a memory is returned to "storage," in a process of *re-consolidation,* that memory will have been changed by the state we were in while the memory was recalled, and by more recent experiences or information. That is one of the reasons why the memories of witnesses in court proceedings must be corroborated – and why a good attorney can change a witness' mind about their own memories.

Time is another variable that influences memory. Things change in the mind with the passage of time, partly due to ongoing changes in the connections between neurons as new data continues to come in, and partly due to changes in the neurochemistry of the brain as we age.

When an event is perceived, it is encoded as a lasting memory in a series of steps. First, the input is interpreted as sensory data in the relevant sensory cortices. For example, when you see something, the visual stimuli is received by the *visual cortex*, and a memory of the object you saw is created. That memory lasts just long enough – often fractions of a second – as an *iconic memory* in the visual cortex to provide for continuity of visual data. That slight persistence of the image is necessary for us to make sense of our world, for example, to notice that a specific object in our visual field has moved.

The visual data is then sent on to short-term memory, which is part of the larger organizational construct of *working memory* (which overlaps both short-term and long-term memory). Attention to the specific sensory stimuli acts like a filter, selecting out what is sent on to short-term memory.

With more filtering for relevance and importance, some memories are sent on from short-term memory to the *hippocampus* for consolidation with other memories and long-term storage. Each type of sensory data is stored long-term in the sensory cortex that originated it, but now marked out by the hippocampus as belonging with memories in other storage locations. In this way, sight, sound, touch, smell, and other memories "know" to activate simultaneously to produce a complete memory when the memory of an "event" is retrieved.

In the process of forming long-term sensory memories, there are three opportunities to forget. If you are overwhelmed with too much visual data coming in and accumulating in the visual cortex before being sent on to the next step in the process, there will be a loss of visual data. This can result in gaps in the memory and in mistaken sequences of data being sent from the visual cortex to the hippocampus. That's the first memory glitch.

The second opportunity for memory loss is during the actual transmission of the data between the visual cortex and the hippocampus. That loss of data can be the result of degraded synapses or injury. Aging can play a significant role in both.

The third opportunity to forget arises when the hippocampus attempts to connect the data with the input of other senses. When the data is incorrectly matched up, the logic circuits of the hippocampus are likely to reject that memory. What you end up remembering is a lot of confusion instead of the actual event itself.

When SWAT teams enter a hostile location, such as breaking through the doors of a felon's hideout, they make use of this capacity for the brain to become overwhelmed and confused. They come in fast and hard with smoke bombs and loud explosions (harmless, of course). They do this to deliberately overwhelm the senses of the unsuspecting occupant. In the debilitating confusion that ensues, the officers can swoop in and take control of the situation and anyone in it.

When the hippocampus has too many things coming at it, it trips a cognitive circuit breaker and stops processing. It's a way to keep the conscious part of the brain from grinding to a halt. That results in gaps in memory, or areas where the memory hasn't been strongly encoded, causing a rapid degradation of the memory (we call it forgetting), or in incorrect remembering. A simple way to avoid this is to stay underwhelmed. In a world that is going at breakneck speed, it seems almost impossible to slow the information coming at us down, but it is possible.

Short-term memories are those memories stored before being sent to the hippocampus for binding for long-term storage. Although filtered by attention, short-term memories, when they can be retrieved, can be more accurate, not yet having been subjected to the same level of interpretation or bias as occurs with long-term memories. Memories that have been transferred into long-term storage by the hippocampus are not just stitched together and associated with other "relevant" memories, they are also bound by neurotransmitters, such as dopamine, oxytocin, and epinephrine, which chemically mark and "color" the memory as "good" or "bad."

Individual long-term sensory memories are stored in the sensory cortices from whence they originated, after the hippocampus has created connections between them and any related memories. Those connections instruct them to activate simultaneously when retrieved later, forming the complete long-term memory.

It takes lots of practice to be able to extract these memories on demand, but it is one of the ways that competitive memory athletes memorize large volumes of data that they then regurgitate accurately. The best way to develop the ability to recall memories from the visual cortex is to train with flash cards. Flashcard training develops the holding capacity of the visual cortex to accommodate larger amounts of visual data, with more robust connections.

Photographic memory

We can't really talk about visual memory without talking about "photographic memory."

In popular culture, the term "photographic memory" is used to describe a camera-like, mythic ability to capture almost instantaneously the memory of a picture or an image in exact detail and composition and to recall it as a perfect replica indefinitely, calling it up like a slide that one can study. That sort of ability is just that, a myth, promoted by entertaining movies and books.

However, there is real "photographic memory," which is very useful, although it is not nearly so dramatic as the stories would have you believe. Real photographic memory is simply the ability to remember visual images or information in great detail.

When we think of photographic memory, we are typically thinking of visual memory, stored in the visual cortex. But photographic memory isn't the exclusive domain of the ocular sense. There are five kinds of photographic memories, each emanating from a different sensory cortex, visual, auditory, and so on.

Photographic memory can exist in the same way for the other four senses as well. It is possible to remember the sequence of sound exactly as it was heard. Someone like Beethoven or Mozart could recreate the exact sound of what they had heard, even playing with it in their minds before reproducing the sounds with a musical instrument. That is a type of photographic memory too, only for hearing.

A person can develop photographic memory as it relates to visual events, or a highly accurate sound memory, or accurate memories based on any of the other senses or combination of senses.

While many people use the phrases "eidetic memory" and "photographic memory" interchangeably, they are not, in fact, the same thing. *Eidetic memory* is the ability to capture a faithful mental snapshot of a sensory event after only a few exposures and to recall it vividly with precision without the help of memory devices or *mnemonics* for some very short time after exposure. Eidetic memory can apply to visual memory or to the other senses. Eidetic memory is rare, something you were either born with or you weren't, and is believed to be found only in children.

In the end, the difference between a photographic memory and a normal memory is one of degree more than it is of kind. It is possible to develop the ability to recall more, because the human brain is built with the capacity to remember more. However, to conserve energy for survival purposes, the brain only records and recalls events it has reason to believe that we need to remember in order to survive. That is one of the reasons that we remember things that threaten our existence more than we remember mundane events or objects.

Memory encoding

The process of encoding memories begins when our senses capture the various stimuli we experience. Each sense we have – sight, sound, smell, taste, and touch – captures packets of information and sends that on to the cortex associated with that particular sense.

Specifically, visual information detected by the eyes is sent to the visual cortex. Sound vibrations detected by the ears are sent to the primary auditory cortex. In a similar fashion, touch, smell and taste data are sent to the sense's corresponding cortex in different parts of the brain.

Those sensory processing regions are located in different areas of the brain for safety. An injury to a specific part of the head might cause a person to lose their eyesight, but their hearing could remain intact, because it is in a different part of the brain. Imagine if data from all the senses were processed in the same place. An injury to that spot would render the person without any sensory input whatsoever.

It should be noted that not all types of memories go through the same process. For example, implicit motor memories do not need the hippocampus for their transfer into long-term memory. Those who have had damage to the hippocampus or have had the hippocampus removed can still learn and remember new motor skills even while they are unable to remember how they learned it, and they aren't able to form any other kind of new long-term memory.

All the different types of sensory data arising from an event don't immediately "sync up" in the brain. Sensory data taken in by the sensory organs is transmitted to the relevant cortices at varying times. In particular, light and sound travel at different speeds. Think about that for a second.

Let's say there is an explosion a thousand yards from where you stand. That explosion generates light, sound, heat, tremors, and smell. Each type of data travels at a different speed. Light travels significantly faster than sound. The light from the detonation will be the first thing to reach the observer, so that is detected first by the eyes. The next to arrive is the sound, faster than any prevailing wind could carry the smell of the ignition material. Finally, the tremor underfoot arrives as the vibration takes time to move through hard material.

The various sensory stimuli from one single event arrive at the observer's different sensors at different times and is therefore recorded by each sensory cortex at different times.

The data from the individual channels is then sent to the brain's hippocampus where the different sensory memories are stitched together into one coherent virtual event. But to do that, the hippocampus needs to recognize all these events as the same event, even though they arrived at different times from different sources. So, the hippocampus accounts for that and holds on to the event in a kind of subconscious memory as all the data is brought together and assembled.

Once you have recorded everything into memory, the next question will be whether you can recall them all and in the correct sequence.

Now, for a moment, let's think of a sports photographer as an analogy. A sports photographer has some really nifty cameras that can capture hundreds or thousands of frames per second. (The world's fastest camera records over 4 trillion frames per second.) When the photographer is taking pictures of a Formula One race, the event consumes thousands of captures. The shutter release button is pressed and thousands of images are captured in just a few seconds. Imagine taking pictures just as a car starts to negotiate a hairpin turn until the car pulls out of the turn – how many ever-so-slightly-different images could there be?

Sporting event photographers take their pictures like this for two reasons. First, they are ready for any mishap or unexpected event that may happen, and they won't miss that vital shot. Second, it provides a bank of a thousand images, and they can pick the best of the lot. Out of a thousand captured frames, it is certain that at least one picture will be perfect enough to hang the moment on.

When the photographer returns to the studio, all the images are laid out and scrolled through to find the best one. The rest are dropped into an archive or just deleted if they are totally irrelevant. Keeping all those unnecessary photos consumes resources. In photography, gigabytes and exabytes of data cost money to maintain in storage.

Like the sports photographer, the senses record thousands of bits of sensory data, thousands of images, for instance. In the brain, storing a unit of memory uses energy, regardless of whether the memory is active or dormant. Just as the photographer goes through the cache of images and chooses what to keep, the brain cycles through the large amounts of data it accumulates during the course of a day, and then encodes for long-term storage the memories it is programmed to keep.

The memory marked out as "important" will get more connections in the brain, while the memory that is not so important will get less. The more neuronal connections the brain makes for a particular memory, the easier the recall process and the longer the memory stays in conscious recall. Memories that are not considered important are still there, but the synaptic paths to get to them are fewer. Deeper thinking is needed to gradually pull those out of storage.

Now let's take this analogy one step further.

Imagine the same Formula One photographer with thousands of images taken at the event. Going through the image cache for the day, the goal may be to find a particular shot that captured a crash, or an image of a particular driver negotiating a bend. Going through the images intent on finding something particular creates a sort of bias. All else is less important. When one is found that tallies with that bias, it is chosen.

Our memory operates in the same way. If we have a certain bias, the memories we keep will be encoded into long-term memory with that bias. We don't just store the raw memory, we store our interpretation of that memory, an interpretation based on our bias.

So, when we look more closely, we start to see that what appears to be a single event is not really the smallest denomination of a memory packet. We see that memory is made up of multiple streams of information stitched together, and that the memory of one event is built one layer at a time from a mosaic of different events.

Those recalled events are virtual, not physical. Think about that for a minute. We get so caught up with reality and our memories of it that we sometimes think that they are one and the same, or that one is the exact representation of the other. With this, we aren't even talking about confusing fantasy and real events. We are just talking about memory, what we remember. We think of it as "real." It is not. It's not even accurate.

Prior memories dictate how we evaluate newer events, how they are interpreted and stored. This is a process that advances forward continuously. All this is done in the hippocampus, where memories are stitched together. When we go to sleep at night, those memories are then permanently recorded in a bioelectrical process of creating neurons and pathways.

No memory exists in a vacuum. This is where any attempt to compare a human memory to a computer hard drive reaches an abrupt limit. While each memory on a hard drive is recorded in a specific address, and that address is recorded in a registry, the human mind places a neuron in the brain, and then connects that neuron to a network of other neurons based on their associative value. Every single neuron can have anywhere from a few to several hundred thousand connections. The more connections, the more entrenched the memory. On a computer hard drive, a memory either exists or it does not, whereas in the human brain, memory exists in degrees.

Chapter 3: Visualization

What it all comes down to is that the mind has its own virtual reality theater, converting what we observe in the real world into virtual representations. A good way to think about this is to compare it with a virtual reality projection. Imagine donning a pair of VR goggles and finding yourself transported into an environment that is not physical in any way, one that is purely light and sound manipulated by software in a hard drive.

In the mind, things are not that much different. We experience things based on our senses, on what we can observe within the limited ranges of electromagnetic radiation we call visible light, of mechanical vibrations we call sound, and of the scents, tastes, and physical sensations that we have receptors for. There is so much more that we are not capable of detecting, yet we remain convinced that what we perceive is the world and that that's all there is.

So, from those limited ranges of sense perceptions, our mind replicates what it has perceived in the real world as a scene in our mind, visualizing our environment. The reason that we are so easily fooled when a reasonably robust virtual reality scenario is placed in front of us is that a VR system only needs to fool our five limited senses. Once it does that, we "believe" what is presented to us.

What does this have to do with memorization?

The primary tool for remembering is visualization. This is not the same kind of "visualization" we usually talk about when we want to achieve something or the kind a star quarterback might use to "see" the touchdown zone in his head as he huddles before the next play. The visualization we are referring to is the way your mind can place the elements of an environment into a virtual space in your mind.

The beauty of visualization is that it works in both directions. You can either see it in the physical world, then recreate it in the virtual world of the mind. Or you can imagine it in your mind, then work to recreate it in the real world – but that is a topic for a different book.

Memory is an integral part of this visualization, and, conversely, visualization is critical to memory.

There is a virtual "you" in your virtual world, with your body, thoughts, and aspirations all part of that intricate virtual world. Everything you do in the real world is intimately connected with what happens in the virtual world.

To illustrate just how important that virtual world is, think back to a time when you were placed in an unfamiliar situation. Can you remember how you felt? Do you remember the strangeness you felt? That sensation of strangeness that comes from being in a new place forces you to look around and quickly assimilate what is out there in order to build up a virtual version of it as quickly as possible, one that you can use to analyze and interact with the world outside.

To drive home the point, now consider an opposite sort of example. Think about the way you feel in a place you are always in. You become complacent. You are so certain of your surroundings that you don't even need to look at things to know what the room looks like and that everything is in place. When you drive to work along a familiar route, you can do it habitually, almost without consciously thinking about every turn – or even actually remembering how you got to the destination.

But what happens when something new is introduced into the real world unbeknownst to you? You may not even see it. There are two kinds of people, the ones who notice even the slightest change in the room, and others who float through their surroundings, not realizing even the largest alterations. The average person has experienced both.

We have varying thresholds for when a change in real environment shakes us out of our reliance on the virtual (remembered) world in our head and forces us to look outside and adjust the internal virtual view. An obsessive person with a rigidly established virtual world may experience terrible anxiety at changes to their real environment, when the real and virtual worlds no longer match.

Once we realize that we have these kinds of virtual environments in our mind, we can start to use them to place stuff into them deliberately. A new memory that is placed into an existing virtual environment (existing memory) will last longer than it would without a place to reside.

To strengthen your ability to visualize environments, start to make a habit of observing your virtual space and your physical space. This takes concentration and the ability to pay attention. Visualize the places you are in, or places that you usually go to, just as you would see them in a Google street view. Look from a bird's eye view then pan down to the street view and look around.

There are many ways to use the brain's natural capacity for visualization and virtualization to strengthen your memory.

Imagine someone giving you directions on the phone, but you don't have a pen and paper to jot it down. How would you remember it? If you are familiar with the place, then you can just mentally imagine the path to the place you need to go to. But what if you are new to the area and you have no idea what the layout of the city is like? You are not going to be able to visualize a map of the area to mentally follow along the path to your destination.

Instead, you can remember the directions by imagining a place you already know, then asking the person who is giving you directions to tell it to you in terms of when to turn left or right. It will be something like "Take the first left, then the third right, followed by the second left." You get the idea.

As you listen to the directions, instead of trying to imagine the area that you do not know, imagine you are in a place that you do know very well. Imagine standing in a familiar spot in your neighborhood. Let's say, you're on the street in front of your house. Now, imagine if you followed the same directions, first left, third right, and second left. Where would that put you in your neighborhood? Can you visualize it? Now you will know exactly where to go – you will be able to remember the path.

Even if you forget the directions, all you'd need to do is think back to how you would get from the familiar spot in your neighborhood to that destination that you are familiar with. Easy.

This simple example demonstrates the technique of taking the unknown and superimposing it onto something that is known in order to remember it more easily.

You can use the same overlapping technique for a different kind of visualization trick you can use to remember numbers, including phone numbers. If you need to remember a number just visualize a typical keypad. The first row, from left to right, are the numbers one, two, and three. The second row is four, five, and six. The third row is seven, eight, and nine. Finally, the zero is in the center of the last row.

To remember a number like 246, just draw the shape the number makes on the keypad. In this case, it makes an inverted triangle starting at 2.

If you have a number like 212-555-2406, can you picture what that would look like if you traced over the number with your finger? The moment you can use your virtual space to trace out this number, you will remember it. You can see your finger dance back and forth for 212, followed by 555 smack in the middle of the keypad. Then 2406 makes a rectangle from 2 to 4, to 0, then back up to 6. Can you see that? The moment you do that, the path your finger traces across the keypad instantly causes you to remember the number in your virtual space.

The idea of visualization is to take something you need to remember and attach it to something that you already have in your mind, an existing memory. That instantly creates a memory and sorts it for recall. The connection between the old and new memory needs to make sense as an association to your brain, not to you. So long as you provide a path to go from A to B, your mind will make the trip.

Visualization works both in memorization and in retrieving memories. Visualization helps both in the recording or encoding of memories, and in their recall.

Chapter 4: Memory Pegs

Human memory is fundamentally associative. Its robustness and flexibility is grounded in the way that new memories are hooked up with older memories. One memory is connected to another and another and another.

Most of what we do and remember is tagged to other things we do and remember. If you see a brown shoe, you will instantly tag it with the color "brown" and the object "shoe." That can trigger a host of other memories. Perhaps your brother owned a favorite brown shoe, which makes you remember the hairstyle your brother had, and that, in turn, reminds you of *The Brady Bunch*. You started with a brown shoe and next thing you know you've travelled down memory lane to *The Brady Bunch*.

That's the "monkey in the brain" doing its thing. Leaping from one branch of memory to another, according to a vast network of associations. You have to love it because it opens up whole new universes, and it allows you to do things that build on what you already know. While it can be a distraction, it is also an asset.

The brain's naturally capacity for association can be used to help you do some rudimentary tasks like remembering numbers and names. Earlier in the book, we described a way to remember phone numbers using the visualization of a keypad. Now, we are going to remember numbers using an auditory association technique. You will be using common easily pronounceable sounds to represent the numbers.

1 = ono (pronounced oh no)

2 = tot

3 = ere (pronounced hey ray)

4 = fof

5 = afa

6 = sis

7 = asa

8 = tat

9 = ana

0 = oh

Here is how you memorize that – in groups of three.

ono tot ere

fof afa sis

asa tat ana

oh

It almost has a lyrical feel to it, which is what makes it easy to remember. Say that a few times, and you will start to be able to visualize the number that each word represents.

Now look at this number: 246.

But, do not call it two, four, and six. Instead, call it, "tot fof sis." All you need to remember is "tot fof sis."

Short numbers are okay, but the benefits become much more obvious when you apply this technique to a long number.

Try it with this one: 337590729.

"Ere ere asa afa ana oh asa tot ana."

Repeat that a few times, and you will find that you remember it much more easily than the numbers themselves.

The reason this works is that the mind not only remembers audio information faster than visual information, it is also more adept at remembering sounds that rhyme or that have vowel-based syllables. In the days of oral history, before the invention of the printing press, ancient orators and storytellers knew this, so when they needed to remember long, long passages, they did it in poetry.

Favorite tunes have been used with children as an auditory pegging device. When a catchy tune that is familiar, while the words are not, is used, new words can be created for material they need to remember. This is a pegging mechanism where you attach the thing you are not familiar with onto the thing that you are already know. So, in this mnemonic device, the tune is familiar, but the words aren't, and when you put them together, it helps you to remember the new words.

More commonly, however, visual pegs are used to attach the things you have just observed to the things you know very well. Making the association allows you to create a permanent memory of the new observation within moments of observing it.

For instance, you can remember phone numbers by pegging them to a phone keypad. Most phone keypads have alphabets grouped to numbers. This can be used to easily remember a phone number. Imagine trying to remember this number, 1-800-287-86637 (not a real number). Can you remember it? If you use the keypad peg, what you get is 1-800-CUS-TOMER. Which is easier? Companies often get phone numbers that can be remembered this way. After all, how effective would a billboard be if they sold you on a product in the three seconds it took to drive past it, but you weren't able to remember their phone number?

So, memory pegs work. You just need to experiment to discover how it works best for you. A little ingenuity goes a long way here. The basic idea is to peg the unknown onto something you know well. By attaching it to an established memory, there is always a way to remember something new.

That is also the essence of how we remember new concepts and how we acquire new knowledge. When you learn something new, you begin by associating names with things. Then you associate the new process to a process that you already know – using analogies and similes. Once that first layer of learning is accomplished, you move on to the next layer, pegging the second layer onto the first. In this way, you gradually build up a block of information in an organized way.

If you combine this sort of pegging with other techniques that keep your mind calm and free of distraction, you will absorb and remember the data better. Although it is the associative qualities of the monkey mind that make memory pegs work, the memory pegs work better when your monkey mind is brought under control.

Memory pegs are easy to use for less important memory tasks like remembering an address for a few moments until you can get to a memo pad or the note app on your phone. There are many ways to do this. You could hang numbers onto the alphabet, associating a word with the number you want to remember. You could add words to a shape to remember the word through the shape.

Suppose you want to remember the address "147 Airport Rd." Start with an easy way to remember 147 just by visualizing it on a keypad as a straight line from top left to bottom left. (Picture the keypad and where the numbers 1, 4, and 7 are located). Then think of an airport you are familiar with. So, all you need to remember is the straight line on the keypad and the airport – and there you have the address. Don't be surprised if you never forget it again.

It takes a little practice at first, but you will get the hang of it. Your mind will adapt to doing things like this as second nature after just a few attempts, because it is your mind's natural way to learn.

Just as you can peg concepts and numbers to familiar memories, you can remember names of people and faces using similar strategies.

The most important thing about a person's name is that it needs to be "attached" to their face. When we say we want to remember names what we really mean is that we want to be able to associate a name with a face. Think about that for a minute. What is the point of remembering "Bob" (the name Bob) without being able to pick Bob out of a group of people? So, the point, again, is to make an association, to find a way to associate the name with the face.

If the name is difficult to pronounce or you haven't heard it before, and you can't even remember the word, you'll have two tasks to accomplish. One is to learn the name and how to say it, and the second is to associate that name to the face. That's not really a memory storage and retrieval issue so much as it is about knowing the pronunciation and getting a completely new word into memory in the first place. The reason foreign names are so difficult to remember is that you don't have a way to peg it onto something you already know. So, you'll need to approach that in a few steps.

Imagine meeting a fellow named Germapolovitch and learning his name once. The first thing you need to do to is remember to pay attention. Most people don't remember names simply because they are multi-tasking instead of paying attention. You need to stop what you are doing, look directly at the person's face, and listen carefully as the name is pronounced. Germ-a-po-lo-vitch. Pay attention to the different elements of the name, the syllables, the stress points, the intonation.

If you ignore all the surrounding inputs and simply concentrate on the name as the person says it, you will remember the sound in your auditory cortex, while your eyes scan his face, remembering that in your visual cortex. If you continue to pay attention, ignoring all other inputs, your brain will have time to move the data into the hippocampus to stitch the auditory and the visual memories together. If you are also smiling when you meet Germapolovitch, feeling happy, the dopamine released will help to bind the memory. If you are upset when you meet him, that works too, because the epinephrine released will also help bind the memory, although categorizing him in the 'bad column' in your memory.

Another trick for remembering a name is to attach a descriptor to it. "Lying Ted" – remember that one? Or, "Crooked Hillary" – hard to forget once you have heard it. For your personal use, use more positive descriptors. Funny descriptors are okay, but disparaging and negative indicators are bad for you, harming you in the long run – not the other person. The technique, however, is very effective.

All these steps take effort, but that's what having a stronger memory is really about, making the effort to remember. Especially when you need to remember a name, a place, a pronunciation, you need to make the effort before it will "stick," because the brain won't waste resources on remembering trivial or unimportant things. It costs energy to remember. When you make an effort to remember, then you'll find that the brain recognizes that "this is important" and will remember it.

In fact, repetition of names and places (or any other thing you want to remember) is really a substitute for attention and focus. It's the harder way, taking more time and effort. However, if you concentrate on just the one thing you want to remember, and cut out all distractions, both internal and external, you will find that you can remember the thing you need to remember much more easily. Whether it's through repetition, or by simply by paying attention, the brain "gets" that the item is important and should be remembered.

Chapter 5: Memory Palace Method

A little earlier in the book, we described a method for remembering directions, which has similarities to the memory palace method we're about to describe. So, let's review that method of remembering directions by overlaying them onto a familiar mental map.

Mentally start at a place on a mental map you are familiar with, but trace the path from one unfamiliar place to another unfamiliar place, according to the directions someone gives you. When the directions are complete, look to see where you have ended up on your familiar map. Then, all you need to do is remember the destination that you are already familiar with.

For example, suppose you are at a gas station in an unfamiliar town. Your client tells you that you need to turn left as you are coming out of the gas station, make a second left, then turn right at the next intersection, and finally turn left again, and then you will find him at the third house on the left. You have no idea where any of this is, and you can't write it down.

So, as he is describing the directions to you, imagine you are at the gas station near your house. Imagining your own familiar mental map, leave the gas station, take a left. Imagine where that puts you on your familiar mental map, then make the second left, and continue following the directions, but superimposing them onto the familiar terrain in your neighborhood.

Suppose that if you were to follow those directions at home, you would find yourself at the Old Donut Shop. So now you have a starting point, the gas station, and the end point, the Old Donut Shop. You won't need a pen and paper because you know exactly how to get to that point – at home. The scenery may be different, the length of each segment may be different, but the sequence, the intangible process memory, is the same. When you attach that intangible process to an existing memory, you can remember what you need to remember. That is also, in essence, how the memory palace method works, by superimposing the unknown onto the known.

The *memory palace* method, or the *method of loci,* is an ancient Roman and Greek technique taught by orators. It uses the visual memory of a physical location or journey as the framework for hanging other information that you want to remember. It takes advantage of the ease with which visual data can be remembered to help retain other material that may be more difficult to remember. It also takes advantage of spatial memory.

In particular, the memory palace method uses the memory power of association and attaches new memories to buildings and places that you have been to or know very well. This is the same theme again – attaching something unfamiliar to something familiar.

The place you chose for your memory palace has to be somewhere you can navigate in your mind fluently without error. You can use an apartment building, a school library, your campus dorm, any place you have a thorough knowledge of. Leave whatever furniture is there that you remember, but you don't have to focus too much on what was there or what wasn't. As long as you can remember the rooms individually, it doesn't matter whether they are empty or furnished exactly – it's about remembering what strikes you.

I use the Tower of London as one of my memory palaces because I've been there many times. It's one of the most conspicuous structures in London and was where prisoners were brought to be incarcerated. Inside the Tower of London, there are many rooms and cells within a vast network of individual sections – which works very well for me as a memory palace. Over time, you can create as many memory palaces as you can use and remember.

Name the rooms in your memory palace according to the way the room makes you feel, or for something like an ornament that makes the room distinctive. You should be able to remember the name easily. For example, the White House's "China Room" is not about the country, China, but about the porcelain plates that are on display in it. The room is named after what is distinctive about it. Do the same thing with the rooms in your own memory palace. You can name them just by adding a descriptor, Stinky Room, Funky Corridor, Blue Stairwell, or whatever makes sense to you.

Once you have created and named the room in your memory palace, you can use it as a framework for hosting things you need to remember. Walk around this building in your mind. Does the name of the room appear to you instinctively? If it does, then you are ready to take the next step, using your memory palace to remember something.

Memory palaces are particularly good for remembering ordered lists or sequences of directions. Have a consistent path to walk through the palace, with repeatable stations or stops along the way. Identify specific spots that you always visit in the same order. If you want, you can also associate each spot with a number. You will use these locations to hang items that you want to recall. For example, if you have a shopping list of nine items, you could mentally walk through your memory palace, stopping at each location, and creating and focusing on creating a clear mental image of the shopping list item in that spot. It's even better if you can make the image memorable, odd, or funny in some way.

How would you use a memory palace to remember the ingredients and steps to make crème puffs – a fairly easy task to start with?

Start with the ingredients. A quart of milk – in your imagination, mentally picture it at your first stop in whatever memory palace you are using. Next, picture the sugar at the next spot, and so one.

To remember the steps in the recipe, you could visual one step at each location in the right order in the memory palace. The more vivid and interesting that you make the image in your mind, the more effective the mnemonic technique will prove itself to be.

As you go through the memory palace process, maintain a feeling of happiness, thinking of how happy your spouse or child is going to be when you surprise them with this dessert, or imagine how happy you will be as you enjoy eating the finished product. The extra emotional oomph will help to bind the memory faster and for a longer time.

By associating the recipe with a highly familiar locations in your memory palace, you will be able to remember that recipe for a very long time, especially after you have actually done it a few times in your own kitchen in the order you rehearsed in your visualization. The process of physically doing something you visualize solidifies and fortifies the memory, adding more layers of neuronal connections to other parts of the brain, a sort of neuronal redundancy.

Chapter 6: The Neuroplastic Brain

Memory and neuroplasticity

If you want to improve your memory, then you will, of course, be dealing with the brain's *neuroplasticity*. Neuroplasticity is the brain's ability to change physically to adapt to new requirements and new situations. When you embark on a quest to create better memory recall, then you are looking for the brain to demonstrate its capacity for neuroplasticity. Whatever mental and memory limitations you may have experienced, whether from illness, stroke, bad habits or choices, the plasticity of the brain means that you can improve from where you are if you decide to and do what is necessary. The brain is moldable and malleable to the point that even stroke victims can be retaught how to do things, rebuilding what was lost through the death of neurons.

I know an eighty-six year old man who lived a good life until he had a stroke on the left side of his brain. It paralyzed him on the entire right side of his body. If he had been one of those people who gives up, that would have been debilitating, making him homebound, at best, or bedridden, at worse. Instead, within eight months, this man was up and about, getting around, and strolling with his walking stick.

What most people don't realize is that a stroke doesn't kill the muscles in the legs and body, a stroke just kills some of the neurons in the brain that are needed to make walking possible. After a stroke, the part of the brain that controls various aspects of mobility in the affected part of the body have been damaged. But, remember, those neurons are not ones you were born with – the brain created them as you learned to walk. After a stroke, those neurons may be damaged and aren't functioning, but that doesn't have to mean that you will never walk again.

The missing neurons can be rebuilt by learning to walk all over again. Learning creates new neurons that are bound together in a coherent way. When you learned to walk as a child, you built neurons and connections that remembered how to do it. As you practiced, your ability to walk developed further, building on those neuronal networks, and every day you walked during your life, you reinforced and built on those memories of how to walk. Even if those neurons are someday destroyed by a stroke, it doesn't mean that you should accept being paralyzed – it can be possible to gradually create new neurons as you regain your ability to walk.

That is the power of neuroplasticity – a brain that can be changed, improved, and even recuperated after injury. That is the kind of memory that really makes a difference in your life. What you remember, whether deliberately or not, literally alters the contours of your brain. What you decide to do in the physical world can physically alter (for better or worse) your brain as the brain builds new circuits, new connections, and new neurons every day. As long as you have the will and desire to do so, you can influence your own brain functioning by doing new things, having new experiences, and thinking in new directions.

To improve your memory by deliberately working with the brain's own natural neuroplasticity, first, you must want to remember. Then you need to pay attention to what you want to remember. These two things are signals to the brain to do what is needed to help you remember. Do that, if you have a healthy brain, and you will be able to remember anything you want. The rest are just tricks – albeit tricks that can make things a whole lot easier.

As for the man who had the stroke, he had a strong will and no fears of whether he would fail or succeed. He believed in his recovery, and acted on his belief, putting in the effort, and, in a few months, he was back on the sidewalk of life. You can do the same thing when it comes to improving your own memory. You may not have had a stroke, but every one of us has been guilty of neglecting our brain. We abuse our brain with things we eat, what we do, bad patterns in life, and with the things we allow into our mind.

In today's world, the same media that can give you information that builds your mind can give you corrosive material that retards it and your mindset. You can choose. You can be the gatekeeper that decides what your own mind is exposed to and consumes. If you choose wisely, you will be rewarded with a powerful mind that allows you to do more than you can imagine. An enhanced memory is just the start of it.

The brain is a robust organ that can develop new neurons and scaffold off old ones rapidly. We are conceived with flawless memory potential, but we lose it as we get older due to inappropriate nourishment, terrible dietary patterns, poor recreational propensities, substance abuse, and so on. All these things can reduce our unique and powerful capacity to create memories and recall them.

Fortunately, the brain was designed to be neuroplastic, so, if you change your habits and adopt a healthy and positive lifestyle, and you practice remembering, recalling and reviewing memories, you will find that your brain will do that more and more easily. In a manner of speaking, we have all had our own little "strokes." We are, on the whole, patients of absent-mindedness, and have reduced our capacity to do what the brain was originally intended to do –

record and retrieve. But we move our brain functioning, and memory specifically, back to doing what it is fully capable of, and recover from these limitations.

To get anything done, including improving your memory, you need to set a goal. Setting a goal tells your brain to do what is needed to achieve that goal. In this case, the goal would be to work on improving your memory, getting it functioning the way it was intended to and is capable of. When you want it, the doors will open for you, the path will become clear. Everything begins with a goal. No direction and no strategy will emerge if you don't have a clear goal, a clear intention.

Exercise: Write out your intention

Get a notepad and a pen. Put them by your bedside. You can also use a stylus and your tablet to replace the book and pen if you like.

This exercise should be the last thing you do each night before you go to bed.

First, you need your specific goal: I WILL HAVE PERFECT MEMORY.

Then, you need the resolve to do it. You need to set your determination, dedication, and resolve firmly into place: I WILL DO EVERYTHING NECESSARY TO ATTAIN IT.

Your statement is broad, but so certain and set that you are telling yourself that you won't let up until the goal is complete. This is the dedication that will take you to success, regardless of what comes across your path. Regardless of what distracts you, you will return to your goal.

Putting them together, now you get this:

I WILL HAVE PERFECT MEMORY & I WILL DO EVERYTHING NECESSARY TO ATTAIN IT.

Write out this sentence 15 times.

This will keep your goal and the direction you want to go fresh in your mind. You don't have to believe it works, just do it. You will find that the other steps you need to take to enhance your memory will fall into place more automatically. It will keep you on track to a better memory.

Continue writing this sentence out every night, indefinitely.

When you do this, you start to get into "the zone." It gets you geared up. It's the kind of thing a quarterback does to rev up to get into the zone to get a touchdown. There are countless people who have used this "trick" to change their lives. This technique is even better for other types of goals, for careers, better lives, and any kind of self-development. You may find yourself astonished by the way you can get something to materialize just by writing it down.

Exercise: Flash photo memory

Unlike other methods in this book for improving memory, this one requires practice and effort. There is no shortcut to practice for building up the skills for a more "photographic" visual memory. This exercise trains your ability to view and "capture" things more quickly, rather than providing a method for memorizing specific material.

For this exercise, use flashcards or an app with a flash card function. Use about a dozen cards for the exercise. Start with cards with simple pictures of objects.

View the cards in rapid-fire sequence. Don't view any card for more than half a second. In other words, flip them at a rate of two cards per second. Never stop to "look" at what is on the card.

You don't want to be consciously trying to analyze and memorize what you see on the car. Your goal is to force your eyes to capture as much as possible in as short a time as possible, without using the verbal and logical parts of your brain.

Have someone hold the cards directly in front of you at eye level. Your focus should be on a point about six inches behind the cards. This will put the face of the card slightly out of focus.

Start flipping the cards. Do not stop even if you think you haven't gotten the information on a card. Just keep going and watch the cards. When you are done, have your partner quiz you on the sequence and content of the cards.

After a few rounds, start using cards with objects with various counts. For instance, the cards may have five balls, four cats, three geese, and so on. The cards should be flashed a little more rapidly this time – at a rate of about three cards per second. Your task is to notice what the object is and how many there are (the count) as the cards are flipped. Once the set is done, you should recall them in the sequence they were shown to you.

Doing these exercises every day will develop your "photographic" memory. You will be more able to quickly see more things in an environment, on a poster, or a person's face – and instantly capture the information that's there.

Exercise: Beethoven's neuron-building Ninth

A simple way to increase neurons and the amount of connections between them is to listen to classical music – and not just Mozart. There is no magic to this. Classical music, especially a symphony, has anywhere from 4 to 100 different musical instruments playing in harmony or in several harmonies to create a composite of sound. At first, your ears hear each individual sound, but the mind only "hears" the overall sound – until you train the mind to translate the auditory stimuli as separate instruments. Having "a good ear" isn't about the capabilities of the physical ear, it's about the attention you pay to the sounds. The more attention you pay, the more detail you will hear.

You can take advantage of the inherent qualities of classical music, listening to it as an exercise to build up and develop the connections between neurons and to trigger your brain into making new neurons, so that your capacity to commit material to long-term memory will be greater.

1. Listen to Beethoven's *Ninth Symphony*

Take some time out to really listen to Beethoven's *Ninth Symphony*. The trick is not just to listen to enjoy it, but to close your eyes and wrap a pair of headphones over your ears. Listen to it at a volume sufficient to drown out outside distractions, and listen carefully to the melody. Listen to all four movements in sequence, because the sequence of the music is also part of the overall effect.

(If you ever happen to be in Vienna, try to attend the Vienna Philharmonic to hear the Orchestra perform the *Ninth*. It is an experience that will change you.)

2. Listen to isolate instruments

Listen to the symphony again, in the same way, with a pair of headphones. This time try to isolate the sounds of the different instruments, and the melody each is playing.

3. Listen for subtleties

Listen to the symphony again, this time looking for other sounds you hadn't noticed before. Move your attention away from the obvious sounds you can hear and listen for more subtle ones. You will find, in time, that you will start to hear new instruments. The overall melody will seem completely different after about the tenth time you have listened to it.

Every single time you do this, you will be making new neurons as your brain learns new auditory material, and building new connections between neurons as your brain makes associations with sounds already encoded into its memory.

The act of sitting still listening to a complex piece of music alters your brain forever. Do this every few days for a week, and you will experience the effects of the brain's neuroplasticity as the way that you think, remember, and feel starts to change.

Chapter 7: Emotion & Memory

Emotions are an important part of our human existence and have a profound role to play in memory and mental functioning. Emotions are actually instrumental in creating memories and in determining their longevity.

One of the most powerful signals in the brain that a memory is "important" and should be saved in long-term memory is a strong positive or negative emotion associated with the memory. The stronger the emotion, the stronger the memory will be encoded, with more connections. Memories are encoded by degree of emotional importance, like a ranking scale.

It is commonplace to think of our heart aching when we are deeply troubled. We think of feelings as coming from the chest, and of rational thoughts as coming from our brain, from our head. While these romantic notions are widely accepted, all of our feelings and cognitive thoughts really come from the same place – our brain.

In the same way that the brain manifests hunger in your stomach, the brain manifests emotional discomfort in your chest. The sensations from your stomach don't really come from your stomach – they come from your brain – but it feels like it's your stomach that is calling for food. In the same way, sensations related to feelings and emotions are activated in the chest. Although that has made it into our language and common expressions, when you say things like "My heart aches," or "My heart is swelling," your heart isn't really doing anything.

You can feel anxiety, stress, and worry physically, in your chest and in the tensing of your back. This emotional response is triggered by the release of *epinephrine* (or *adrenalin*), a major cause of the jitters during periods of anxiety. It turns out that one of the key hormones responsible for the creation of long-term memories is epinephrine. It is the triggering of epinephrine during frightening situations that helps to create crystal-clear memories of fear-filled situations.

Now, let's look at this in reverse. If epinephrine is responsible for making strong long-term memories, consider what happens when you take a beta-blocker, a medication that inhibits the uptake of epinephrine. Since beta blockers block epinephrine, the formation of long-term memories can also be affected, and you may start having memory problems. If you are on beta-blockers, you can attest to this side-effect after taking them for some time.

However, if you have been prescribed beta blockers, then you shouldn't stop taking them without consulting your doctor, even if your memory is deteriorating. But if you are not already on beta blockers, then you may want to discuss alternatives with your doctor before taking these kinds of medications.

We especially remember things that cause us immense pleasure or immense pain. In cases of anxiety, epinephrine is released, and a strong memory is formed. On the other hand, memory is also reinforced with the release of *dopamine*, another key *neurotransmitter* in the formation of memories. Dopamine is a powerful "feel good" neurotransmitter that rewards us for doing the activity that triggered its release. Memories encoded with a dopamine release have a happy bias, while ones encoded with an epinephrine release have the opposite tone. We remember immense pain to help us avoid it in the future, while we remember immense pleasure so that we will want to repeat whatever caused it. Remembering pleasure and pain is how the brain manages our experiences.

Oxytocin is another neurotransmitter that is important for memory. Oxytocin, sometimes referred to as the love neurotransmitter, causes us to remember who we love, and even creates that feeling of love. This type of emotional memory is a huge part of our lives. It bonds us with our mates, children, and other family members. It provides the feeling of the assurance we need as we grow up under our parents' protection. It provides strong connections as we form our own communities. Loving emotional memory gives us structure and strength in our social circles, and it contributes to the cohesion we need for a happy society.

Understanding how emotions and neurochemistry strengthens memories and makes them last, you can use this knowledge to design strategies that will result in longer lasting memories when you want to. You can also choose to become more careful about creating negative memories that you might not want to keep or reinforce. For example, you might start to avoid saying or doing anything that escalates a situation when tempers or fears flare. Bad experiences can become emotional baggage, so be careful what you commit to memory.

Emotional memory is powerful, so try not to go down roads that create negative memories that you'll have to deal with in the future. If you are in a situation that is about to turn ugly walk away and save yourself the unpleasantness of carrying that memory around for a long time to come. Reduce your stress, walk away from strife, and learn to calm your mind. This will improve your memory in more ways than you can imagine.

On the other hand, create more good memories, and spend time making memories with those you love and those you want to be close to. Do things in different places and meet new people. All these things will give you the opportunity to make new positive memories. These pleasurable and positive memories will create a better (and more pleasant) cerebral environment for processing and binding memories. If you are happy, more of your memories will be happy too. The momentum of emotional memory created by lots of positive memories will make you a happy person, and you will be more adept at making new positive memories.

Around and round it goes.

The memories held most strongly in our brain help to dictate our emotional reactions, and our emotional reactions help indicate to our brain what we should remember most strongly and clearly. When we understand this cycle, and the cycle is a positive one, we can use that to our advantage to reinforce the things we want to remember. When the cycle is a negative one, we can start to disrupt it, and begin to remember more of what we want to remember.

Chapter 8: Mindfulness, Meditation, and Reflection

Earlier, the way that becoming overwhelmed interferes with memory acquisition was described. Instead, if you can keep yourself from being overwhelmed, the process of transporting memories of events to the hippocampus can occur without a hitch. Information from the various cortices of the brain – each handling data from a different sensory organ – can then be effectively bound together in the hippocampus.

If you can keep the stream of data being processed constant and consistent, then all the parts of the brain, from the cortices to the hippocampus, are going to work together synchronously. However, if too much data is coming in, or if the data is coming in from irrelevant sources, then the binding mechanism will be thrown out of sync.

Imagine observing a firecracker that has both a loud bang and a bright flash. If you experience it close up, you will perceive that bang and the flash as happening at the same time. But how can that be? Because sound travels slower than light, the flash should reach you first, and the sound should reach you later. But you remember the sound and the flash as being simultaneous. Why?

The brain binds the data from an event in a logical way, based on previous experiences, and according to the logic that sensory data arising from an event happened at the same time.

On the other hand, what happens when the senses are faced with widely separated timing between inputs? What if the bang and flash occurred so far away that the flash was obviously seen first and the bang was clearly heard a little later? Why doesn't the mind rectify that? Because logic says that it is too far for the sound to arrive at the same time the flash does.

There is a logic circuit at play when the hippocampus is working to bind the different memories and sensory inputs of an event together. If the sequence of events doesn't seem logical based on past experiences, the experience will seem "off" or "weird," and the hippocampus tends to discard the newly bound memory.

Mindfulness and the "monkey mind"

Becoming overwhelmed by too much chaotic input makes it difficult for the hippocampus to bind memories together correctly. However, if you move at the speed of your memory, that is to say, if you slow things down, and you don't occupy the mind with too many things at once, then you can get a detailed capture of all the things that are going on around you. And that is the art of mindfulness.

Mindfulness is the practice of purposefully focusing the attention with an open and non-judgmental attitude. Focusing on your senses in the here and now is one common approach to being mindful.

To pay attention is to successfully avoid distraction. To avoid distraction requires a solid selection process of what is relevant and what is not. That's the foundation. Being someone who has top memory starts with selecting out what is relevant from what is not, then purposefully paying attention to what is relevant.

If you develop a state of mindfulness in all you do, paying attention to what you are doing and where you are, you will find that the brain is able to remember everything you need it to. The key is to make mindfulness a habit. When you do that, you create the foundation for a stronger memory. In fact, mindfulness is an important ability for an efficient brain, in all it does.

To understand mindfulness, it is helpful to think of your mind as being made up of three parts. The first part of your mind is constantly cycling through thoughts, like a movie that is always playing in your head – a very disconnected and fleeting movie. This is what's often referred to as the "monkey mind" because your thoughts jump around like a bunch of monkeys swinging and leaping erratically from branch to branch.

The second part of your mind is quieter. It goes about its present task, seeking out information and accessing learned skills to accomplish it. This is cognition.

You could call the third part the "umpire." It observes the other two parts and decides what to do. This third part also has a lot of other inputs to take into account – the primitive mind with its basic urges, for instance. The umpire passes its recommendations on to you. ("You" are not your mind.)

Mindfulness occurs when you have aligned the three dimensions of your mind – the monkey, the cognitive side, and the umpire – and they are all aligned in the moment, purposefully paying attention to the same thing, calmly, and with an attitude of acceptance and nonjudgment.

Let's look at common experience, as an example, to illustrate this. Imagine being in a movie theater watching a movie, and your monkey mind, your cognitive mind, and the umpire are all trained on the events on the screen – you are being mindful of the movie. Suddenly, an unruly patron is making a fuss two rows ahead. Your cognitive mind is probably still trying to watch the movie, but your monkey mind has been knocked off its movie-viewing perch and is coming up with all sorts of thoughts about the noisy patron. That gives the umpire two feeds of data – and one is not relevant to the other.

So, now, there are two sources of stimuli: the story on the screen, and the noisy patron. Mindfulness is picking one or the other. It might seem obvious that you should choose the movie, but that is not the point. The point is to pick one, so that all faculties of the mind are trained and focused on that one thing. Which you choose to focus on is really a separate consideration of the benefits you will receive. There are certainly situations where paying attention to the patron might make more sense in the moment.

However, let's assume that you know right off that focusing on the unruly patron will give you nothing but angina, whereas focusing on the movie will give you what you paid for – pleasure. So, you make the choice to return your attention to the movie – but your monkey mind doesn't agree. It wants to continue cussing out the unruly patron.

The question now becomes how to bring the monkey mind back into unified focus with the cognitive mind. Generally, you need to distract the monkey mind with something else. You need to give it something different to attract its attention, because, until you do, it is in the nature of the monkey mind to bring up associated thoughts called up by whatever has caught its attention.

If you wait a minute or two, and there is another exciting scene on the screen, that should be enough to capture the monkey's attention, and it will get back to watching the movie. Otherwise, a good way to do it might be to head out to the concession stand to get a drink and more popcorn. By the time you get back, the monkey will have forgotten all about the earlier distraction.

In a long and roundabout way, this illustration highlights something that you need to understand about the composite mind. Your mind has a variety of functional areas that are each there for a reason and with important roles to play.

The part we have been calling the "monkey mind" is a crucial part of brain and memory functioning, vital to the survival and functioning of the whole being. The apparently chaotic "monkey mind" is the visible outcome of the brain working by association. It is the result of the brain being triggered by an external (or internal) stimulus to identify as many associated memories as possible to relate the new event to something that already exists in the brain.

Associative memory is fundamental to the functioning of your brain. Without it, we would not remember anything. One of its roles is to keep you safe, which is why it is so adept at pulling up negative thoughts and memories. You need the associative part of your mind. If you didn't have it, you would not be able to trigger thoughts based on your external environment.

However, when you need to stay focused and pay attention so that you can remember everything, you need that associative part of your mind to align itself with the other parts of your mind in a single stream of consciousness. If there is a conflict between your cognitive processes and your "monkey mind," then your thinking is not cohesive, and it becomes difficult to keep a memory record of what is going on internally or in the physical world.

Mindfulness brings everything back into focus on one stream. Through regular practice, you attach your thoughts to the things you want them to be associated with. The way you start your day is important. Mindfulness practice is especially powerful in the morning. When you wake up and feed your mind calmness and positive messages, it tends to stay that way for more of the day because the associative function of the brain seeks out related things.

Feeding the monkey with positive stimuli when you wake up makes it easier to stay mindful. Then, even if you do encounter that rude person in the cinema, the monkey isn't going to put up as much of a fuss. So, your first step toward mindfulness is to start your morning off right so that there is more agreement between the monkey, the cognitive mind and the umpire.

You should also keep a check on your mental consumption habits, on what you put into your mind. If it's a lot of garbage, you can't expect to be as sharp as you need to be in order to be mindful and remember things well. Gratuitous violence on TV, video games, and gossip are just some of the unlimited number of things that can affect the associations your mind makes. These are all distractions the mind can do without – and when it does, you will find its ability to be mindful is that much stronger.

The more mindful you can be in any moment, the more you will remember of it. Whether it is a phone number or the nuanced facial tick of a person's nonverbal response as you say something, you will find that with a clear and mindful mind, you will be able to observe and remember more of it.

Practice silencing the monkey mind at least once a day by removing yourself from all external stimuli. During that time, do not look for anything to think about. It isn't a time for you to reflect. It isn't a time for you to ponder or work stuff out. It is a time for you to simply allow the turbulence of your mind to settle down.

Remember that the monkey mind is always reacting to the surroundings – and you do want that sometimes. But, to practice mindfulness, you need to remove the external stimuli and get the mind to calm down on its own. You need to give that monkey a break.

So, as after you drop a pebble into the water in a bucket, ripples will spread outward, then turn at the walls of the bucket to return back inwards, colliding with more outward-moving ripples. The result is a lot of apparent chaos. In the same way, when the monkey is given a stimulus, the ripples in the mind propagate across associated neurons to trigger other thoughts. Those thoughts trigger yet other associations, and it goes on and on. But, if you can stop the original stimulus, eventually you can stop the mind from bouncing up against itself.

That is why you need to choose a quiet spot to allow the mind to settle. When you drop that pebble into the bucket of water, after a while, what happens to the ripples? For a while, they bounce around, interfering with each other, creating some chaos, but then eventually the ripples dissipate, and the water settles down into such a state of calm that you could even see a reflection of yourself in it.

This calm state of mind is the best time to expose it to whatever you want to remember. If it seems like a long way to go to remember something, you are not wrong. It can take time to get the mind to calm down, especially when you haven't practiced it.

There is one more thing you can do, besides secluding yourself, to alleviate the constant barrage of distractions. Simply stop energizing the monkey. How? Don't pay attention to it. When you pay attention to those seemingly random thoughts, you end up fueling them. The more you pay attention, the more the "monkey mind" goes in search of even more associations.

Paying attention to those associations is like dropping more pebbles into the bucket, so that the ripples never really dissipate. Paying attention is like providing resonance to a pendulum in a clock. As long as the resonating mechanism is active, the pendulum will never stop swinging back and forth. With that in mind, then, simply take some time to stop the outside stimuli, and stop giving attention to whatever the monkey mind offers up, and you will find that your thoughts will gradually calm down.

If you have mindfulness practice sessions every day, you will gradually find yourself increasingly able to bring your mind into a calm state. With practice, you will be able to bring your mind to a state of calm quickly, if you start the session by taking three deep cleansing breaths. Do this every day, and, over time, your mind will develop a habit of associating three breaths with a calm mind. Eventually, you will just need to take the three deep cleansing breaths, and your mind will instantly calm and enter a focused and undisturbed state.

In this calm state, it will be easier to remember anything you want. It is the best way to focus the mind, but it takes time to practice. Don't give up.

Breathing and calming the mind has other benefits too. It allows the mind to concentrate at will and increases the power of your mind. But for now, your only interest is to get it to remember.

If you make this calm mindfulness your usual state, you will be surprised at how much better you remember the details and nuances of everything that happens around you. Whether you are in a classroom attending a lecture, or in a conversation with a loved one pouring out their heart to you, whether you are walking through a forest alone, or sitting in a cheering crowd, you will be better able to observe what is important, remember it, and understand it.

Meditation

As much as they are often linked, meditation and mindfulness do very different things. Mindfulness provides the environment to silence the monkey. Meditation is about a completely different dimension of change. Without considering the potential spiritual dimensions of meditation, the physical effects of meditating can be profound. Not only does practicing meditation provide all sorts of overall health benefits, it also physically changes the functioning of the brain – and that results in altered thought patterns.

There are many ways you can meditate, but meditating to improve your memory and ability to recall can be very simple. It doesn't require any fancy ritual.

Find a suitable place where you can sit down without being disturbed. Get comfortable and go through your mindfulness exercise.

When you feel calm enough, start to focus on the silence. Do not interact with any sounds or thoughts that might intrude on or interrupt your silence. Simply be patient and do not get caught up with the thoughts or sounds. Continue sitting there, and just watch all the thoughts as they go by. Do not react to them. Neither accept them nor fight them. Do not even give them a second thought. You can just sit back and allow your thoughts to settle on their own.

The best way to do this is to imagine watching a movie. Have you ever ended up being so engrossed in the movie that you felt that there was nothing else in the room? You were almost in the movie. Right? But, then, there's a knock on the door, and you snap out of your oneness with the movie, breaking the illusion of being in it. After you get rid of whoever was at the door, you return to your movie, but you are no longer in it, and you are distinctly aware that you and the movie are separate from each other.

Meditation is like that – in reverse. When you meditate, you actually will yourself to step back from the processes of the mind. You step back and observe the cogitation of the mind and the monkey in the mind. It takes practice, but the benefits are amazing. When you pull yourself back from your thoughts and the activities of your mind, you lift yourself out of "street view" into an "aerial view" of your own thoughts, yourself, and your surroundings – it's like going from a "street view" to an "aerial view" on Google Maps.

The process of meditation, when you pull back from your own consciousness, results in a greater ability to arrange neurons and their connections, and to reduce clutter in the mind. Scientists who have studied the brain with sensors have detected heightened electrical activity in the brain.

But isn't meditation supposed to calm the mind? That seems contradictory, but it isn't. Meditation is not meant to make us placid and calm. Meditation is not a tool to dull the mind. Meditation organizes the activities of the brain, making the mind more clear and alert.

Meditation changes the way you create memories, taking advantage of the neuroplasticity of the brain, realigning neurons in a more organized way, arranging them in groups that are more coherent. That's what you are doing when you step back and watch your mind. Something almost magical happens when you meditate –

which forces the brain to reorganize its neurons and make them more efficient and effective in their connections and clarity. When you meditate, it alters the way your brain makes associations, and, so, your memories become more organized.

How does this help?

When you have random thoughts zipping all over your mind – which is how the associative brain is supposed to work – sometimes, the distraction it creates can be debilitating. Ask anyone who has had to deal with that as part of life. Imagine what a chaotically-arranged mind does to you. Imagine what the associative quality of memories seems like at that point. It can be confusing, frustrating, even debilitating.

To increase your memory skills, quieting these associative bursts will go a long way toward being able to memorize things faster, and binding those memories more effectively.

Meditation helps arrange those neurons (representing bundles and fragments of data) into nice little bundles in ways that you can't physically do. Meditation is like defragging the brain. Have you ever done that on a computer? Defragging basically takes all the files that have become scattered across the hard drive in different sectors and locations, which makes the location of the information incoherent, and rearranges it all so that the information is neatly organized, making the retrieval of information more efficient.

Meditation takes a little time to master, and it takes a little more time to see the benefits. Typically, it takes about six weeks to really notice the benefits, when you will notice a better ability to focus and concentrate. In particular, you will notice that it creates a "silence" as the monkey in the mind becomes less intrusive.

Reflection

Reflection and contemplation helps to clear the cobwebs from your mind and to remove the corrosion that troubles your psyche. The ideal approach to contemplation is simply to ignore the chaos – anything that upsets the monkey.

The key is to center your thoughts on the silence that resides deep within you. All of us have a silent center in our mind. Upon that silence, all noise and chaos are built. When you center on that silence, the mind, cognitive or associative, has nothing to record, the turbulence in the mind begins to calm, creating a conducive environment for powerful insights.

Inside that silence, you will be able to start reflecting on yourself and the resolutions you need to make. Make no mistake, reflection is the only way that you can put to sleep all the ghosts that haunt your mind and distract your efforts for a better memory. Reflection puts to bed all that is unnecessarily vexing your mind and soul, allowing your mind to focus on what you want. That helps you retrieve everything you want to remember. Once you have recorded a memory during a state of mindfulness, all you'll need to do is enter a state of contemplation, and search for the material that you want to ponder.

When you combine mindfulness, meditation, and reflection, you get nothing short of a life-altering change that happens at the seat of decision-making.

Frequency

At its most fundamental level, the brain is a bioelectrical organ. The neurons are constantly sending pulses of electricity that travel rapidly across the brain. That rapid pulsing creates a rhythm – a frequency. This frequency can be measured by the cycles it makes and ranges between 0.5 Hz and 90Hz.

The lower frequencies occur when you are asleep, while the highest are generated during states of excitement. During sleep, your frequency ranges between 0.5 and 4 Hz – that is called the *delta* state. The *theta* state is above that, between 4 and 7 Hz, and is the range of your subconscious mind, the dreamy state you feel under extreme drowsiness.

Just above that is where the best learning and memory creation occurs, the *alpha* state, with frequency ranges between 7 and 12 Hz. This is also where you brain rests in a state of meditation and mindfulness. In the alpha state, memories are encoded with greater accuracy, and they last longer. If you practice meditation on a daily basis, this is the state that you can be perpetually in.

Deeper meditation slows brain frequencies more, falling into the theta state of deep relaxation.

Chapter 9: Fading Memory, Diet, Exercise, and Sleep

In a healthy person with healthy habits, memories fade for one (or both) of two reasons. The first is that the memory wasn't formed strongly enough when it was first created. For example, something may not have been noticed or observed clearly enough to begin with. The second reason is that the memory hasn't been used in a long time and so the connections to that memory have degraded over time.

Those are the "soft" (as in "software") reasons for fading memory, but there are also "hard" (as in "hardware") reasons for memory loss, physical reasons that have to do with chemistry, biology, and physics.

Sometimes forgetting things isn't just about bad memory. Sometimes mini-strokes you aren't even aware of cause neurons to die off. If you find you have really forgotten something, you should retrain your mind to remember it, thereby getting your brain to reconstruct those neurons and connections.

Memory erosion can happen because of bad habits that retard brain activity. If you are not keeping yourself healthy and you have bad habits that keep you in a suboptimal state then you will find that your memory will gradually deteriorate. You will eventually get to a point where it is not easy to encode a memory, and, even when encoded, it won't last long.

Eating and drinking

The more the mind needs to maintain memories, the more energy it takes. Memories do degrade naturally over time. It requires energy to be able to maintain all of them. You will notice that children in poorer neighborhoods have a hard time learning. Poor nutrition is often the culprit. The brain uses a lot of energy and nutrients in forming the memories needed in learning.

If you supply your brain with a constant and stable source of energy, you will find that you are more alert and able to remember more. The best way to improve memory is to eat a diet that provides your brain with the stable energy it thrives on. When your mind is fully energized, the process of creating memories and binding them becomes extremely proficient.

The human species evolved on a diet high in proteins and fats, with a metabolic process that is very different than the average diet of the western world. The human brain evolved to thrive on a diet that relies heavily on using triglycerides (fats) and fatty acids as fuel rather than carbohydrates and glucose.

The point is to feed the brain with energy supplied as 80 percent ketones (a by-product of the metabolism of fat) and 20 percent glucose. To do this, the body needs to start burning fat for fuel instead of glucose or glycogen. This is not as simple as changing your diet; it requires a new way of eating and a few days to change your body's metabolic system. Your best bet is to get on an Intermittent Fast and High Fat Diet. A little bit of research or a book on the subject of ketones will help to understand how you can make that work for you.

Don't forget to drink plenty of water, making sure to maintain a good balance of electrolytes. Being even slightly dehydrated can quickly impair brain function and memory. Water is essential for delivering nutrients and for removing toxins. Drinking more water is quite simply the easiest way to boost the performance of your brain and memory. Electrolytes and salts are important too – remember that a functioning memory depends on the electrical impulses that jump across synapses, something that cannot happen without salt and electrolytes.

Once you have your basic dietary issues taken care of, you need to look at your other habits. Two things that are not good for your brain are substance abuse and mental stress. Mental stress is greatly helped by mindfulness and meditation. Excessive alcohol, drug, and nicotine use can be more challenging, but, to have a strong and precise memory, you need to be able to stay away from those toxins and habits. Small amounts are easily handled by the body, but toxins that remain in the system after long-term use can be a problem. Also, as much as possible, stay away from processed foods, flavor enhancers like MSG, and artificial sweeteners. If you can do all this, you will find your memory starting to get better, and your ability to retain and recall memories will improve.

Working out

The brain is a resource hog and needs lots of oxygen to keep functioning. If you have ever been in an oxygen chamber, you will know how much different it feels to have lots of oxygen.

Some years ago, I participated in some high altitude training at Andrews Air Force Base where they have chambers that simulate high altitude, low-pressure environments. I already knew that lack of oxygen reduces the efficiency of the mind, but the crew teaching the course also demonstrated that, when there is decompression and lack of oxygen, not only do the eyes lose their ability, but the brain fails to recognize that it is not working properly, and descends into a sense of false well-being and silliness. When we put on the oxygen masks, the mental fog lifted in an instant. Only then did we realize that there was any difference. We had not realized what a state of diminished mental ability we had been in. The difference between the state of being oxygen deprived and being in an oxygen-rich environment was pronounced – the brain instantly perked up and was alert once again as soon as we had more oxygen.

Oxygen is the key to increase mental capacity physically, and you should do what you can to increase your oxygen saturation. Generally, we live our lives without any idea whether our oxygen saturation is high or low, but we don't need to don masks to get more oxygen. The best way to increase your oxygen levels, shy of plugging yourself up to an O2 canister, is to work out regularly to increase your pulmonary efficiency and your hemoglobin count. If you work out regularly, at least once a day, you will increase your oxygen intake and blood oxygen levels. That will help your brain function and repair itself if there is an injury you are unaware of. More oxygen will make all the difference to your mental functioning and to your memory.

As a bonus, the endorphins (feel-good neurochemicals) you get from working out are also good for the brain and will keep you in a good state of mind long after you finish the workout session. They will help keep you alert, your mind calm, and your ability to remember in top shape.

Sleep

Finally, you need to pay more attention to your sleep and wake cycles. Try not going to sleep for 48 hours, and you'll start to feel the psychological and manic effects, and the memory impairments caused by a lack of sleep. Remember, your day doesn't start when you wake up and end when you go to bed. It starts when you fall asleep and it ends when you fall asleep again.

Personalizing your sleep habits to get the right sleep for you is the best way to prepare your mind for better memory, and to have a powerful and active mind. There are three elements to incorporate into your sleep plan for supercharging your powers of retention and recall. The first is to get the right amount of sleep. The second is to get up before dawn. And, finally, it is to have specific routines for the hour before going to sleep and the hour after waking up.

1. The "right" amount of sleep

The "right" amount of sleep varies from one person to the next. There are too many factors to accurately dictate the amount of sleep time you need. But you can discover that for yourself through "experiment." You need to invest in a little effort and record-keeping to discover what your own unique best sleep period should be.

What you are looking for is to wake up without any memory of a dream. Those who wake up in the middle of a dream have not fully completed their sleep cycles. Each of us goes through sleep cycles throughout the night, usually about two sleep cycles. If you finish a full cycle, you feel refreshed and alert. If you wake up in the middle of the first cycle, or even the second, you will feel lethargic and groggy.

Keep a journal to record the time you go to bed and the time you wake up with an alarm clock. Also note whether you have any memory of a dream as soon as you wake up. No need to recount the dream. Markdown these times. Monitor and record the total amount of sleep time you had on the days that you had no memory of a dream – vague dreams don't count.

Experiment with varying amounts of sleep until you have awoken on a number of days with no memories of a dream. Average the number of hours of sleep you got on those days that you didn't recall any dream.

Once you have that average number, then that is what you should aim for as your sleep cycle. Work backward on the clock from 5 a.m. to find the time that you should go to sleep. For example, if you find that you have a seven hour optimal sleep time, then mark off seven hours before 5 a.m. That's 10 p.m. That means you need to start your sleeping ritual by 9 p.m. and then drift off to sleep by 10 p.m.

2. Early to rise

The second item is simple. Get up before the sun and you will find that your day goes really smoothly – it's not luck, it's that your brain is in the right gear for the day and so you are able to handle everything in a way that feels smoother. In fact, many elements that favor early morning rising go into human sleep rhythms, including hormones such as melatonin (which regulates sleep-wake cycles). We have naturally evolved to respond to the bluer light of morning by "waking up" for the day, becoming more alert, with all systems set to "go."

3. Rituals before & after sleep

You want to develop rituals for the start and end of your sleep cycle. These rituals are so that you set yourself into a state that helps you get to sleep. It is the same reason you get your kids into a certain kind of pajamas and go through a series of actions before going to bed – you can't just get them from the TV to bed – they will have poor sleep. You will too. So the hour before you sleep and the hour after you wake up are times that you will do the following ritual.

For your bedtime ritual, choose a specific chair and a specific time. Include breathing and meditation in your bedtime ritual. This time is private and yours alone – it is not a time for chit-chat or conversation. You could also do this as a buddy ritual, with you and your spouse doing this together. Just before you fall asleep, have a glass of water next to you and drink exactly half of it and fall asleep.

When you wake up, start your morning ritual by drinking the remaining half of the glass of water, and sitting in your special chair meditating about the morning, the day ahead, and the things that you are going to observe and remember during the coming day. Affirm to yourself that you are in control, that you are observant, and that you will do whatever it takes to remember. You can add to this another affirmation that you seek first to improve your life, and, after this, you should get to your morning workout.

Having begun your day, refreshed with enough of the right kind of sleep, you will find that you are in top shape to spend your day actively building memories that you can effectively remember whenever you need or want to.

Conclusion

There you have it. By this point, you should have a better appreciation of your brain, the mind that it gives rise to, and the mystery of memory. Memory is at the heart of all the things that you are and do. It is a central feature of everything that makes us human.

This book has given you several different threads that you can pull on to develop your own best strategy for improving your memory and your overall mental functioning.

The brain does three things – it interprets, it processes, and it remembers. External and internal stimuli trigger the need to interpret, process, and then remember. That body of remembered data then exerts influence over new data coming in. As a newborn child, looking at a table didn't immediately result in you knowing that it was a table. You didn't even see what we, as adults, see. It is only over time, as visual memory is recorded, and the features and uses of the table are experienced, that we develop in our memory a profile of the table and what it is used for.

To understand the sheer magnitude of the human memory, imagine a flight data recorder in a commercial jetliner. It records a number of flight parameters in a 90 minute loop. At Time 91, it starts going back over itself to record new data. That data never gets used or accessed unless there is a catastrophe and investigators want to understand what happened. The information includes a cockpit voice recorder that records all communication and sound that occurs in the cabin, plus all the movements of critical flight controls. Flight officials can plug that data into a computer and look at a simulation of what the plane was doing for up to 90 minutes prior to the accident or incident.

That is a lot of data even if it is only 90 minutes. But that is only a miniscule fraction of the data carried in the human brain. We store everything from the moment of the first neuron's creation until death – and we access much of it over and over, at different times, for different reasons, using it in a multitude of different ways.

The brain is the world's largest capacity memory storage unit. The limits of its capacity have not yet been discovered. You can retain everything you are exposed to in one form or another. You have it all there. If you access the memory of what happened in the long-term memory network, you will find that the memory is tinged with the interpretations you made of it back then, prejudices, biases, and all. The brain is no mere data storage device like the plane's black box.

Although we often liken our brain to a computer, it really isn't like one beyond a few over-simplified concepts. Instead, there are quantum devices, logical circuits, and tremendous amounts of back up and associative references in our brain, allowing us to have more robust abilities than any computer or even supercomputer. If you leave the world's most powerful supercomputer turned on, it will stay in that same state forever, but a child will observe and learn. The child will use its memories to create more experiences and test more scenarios, changing itself, its environment, and its own brain in the process.

We have been describing our associative mind as a "monkey in the brain" to the extent that the mind is constantly jumping from one branch to another – and that's just what we are conscious of. In reality, the mind jumps many more times and much faster than we could ever be aware of as it samples every area of the brain in search of the next associated thought. If you were conscious of all that sampling, you would immediately become overwhelmed. The awesome power of our mind and memory is rooted in this constant associative dance in our human brain.

The philosophy behind this book has been to provide you with the understanding you need to improve your memory right here, right now, where you stand. You don't need to take any supplements or concoctions or have any implants put in. All you need to do is to activate the existing internal structures of the brain you already have. It takes desire, and a determination to learn new things, to create new networks of neurons, and even trigger neurogenesis.

That's it. Now, take what you have learned and go make some positive memories. Avoid creating bad memories, and always work to set things right so you won't be haunted by memories or feel afraid to venture down your own memory lanes. If you remember more, and make your memories better, it can change your life.

If you enjoyed learning how to hack your mind and improve your memory, I would be forever grateful if you could leave a review. Reviews are extremely important for authors to help us boost our creditability. It also helps your fellow readers find the books worth reading so make sure to help them out!

www.ingramcontent.com/pod-product-compliance
Lightning Source LLC
Chambersburg PA
CBHW030051100526
44591CB00008B/110